the techniques of *judo*

the techniques

charles e. tuttle company:

of ***judo***

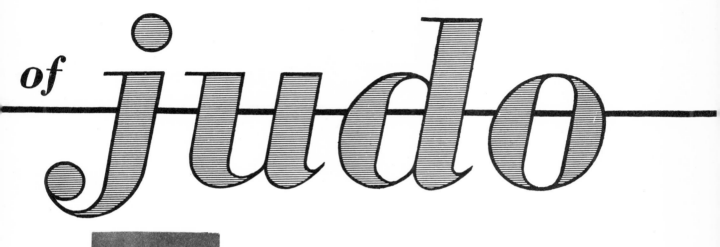

by

shinzo takagaki &

harold e. sharp

publishers: rutland, vermont & tokyo, japan

Representatives

For Continental Europe:
BOXERBOOKS, INC., *Zurich*

For the British Isles:
PRENTICE-HALL INTERNATIONAL, INC., *London*

For Australasia:
PAUL FLESCH & CO., PTY. LTD., *Melbourne*

For Canada:
M. G. HURTIG LTD., *Edmonton*

Published by the Charles E. Tuttle Company, Inc.
of Rutland, Vermont & Tokyo, Japan
with editorial offices at Suido 1-chome, 2-6, Bunkyo-ku, Tokyo

Copyright in Japan, 1957 by Charles E. Tuttle Company, Inc.

Library of Congress Catalog Card No. 56-13413

International Standard Book No. 0-8048-0569-5

First edition, 1957
Fifteenth printing, 1970

PRINTED IN JAPAN

foreword

the number of judo-men who, in the past eighty years since judo became established as a sport, have succeeded in really mastering the sport of judo have been few indeed. Fewer still, however, have been the men who, like Mr. Shinzo Takagaki, *kyu-dan* (9th grade) and author of the present volume, have not only mastered the sport but have also proven themselves as outstanding instructors, with a genuine understanding of the problems that face the students of judo. Mr. Takagaki's first contact with the sport came at the early age of twelve, when he first started practicing, and he has kept up his interest and enthusiasm for the sport to this day. After graduating from Nihon University in Tokyo in 1923 he went to the U.S.A. for higher studies. Much of his time was spent practicing and teaching judo while in America and subsequently while he was in Canada. Ever since then he has devoted a large part of his time and effort to propagating and aiding the growth of judo abroad. He was largely responsible for getting the sport started in India, where he founded the Tagore University Judo Institute. He introduced the sport in Nepal and Afghanistan where he received the highest decoration of that country for his efforts. After the Second World War he toured a number of South American countries as head of the official Kodokan Judo Delegation.

As his career amply demonstrates he has contributed perhaps more than any other individual to the growth of the world-wide enthusiasm and interest the sport of judo commands today.

When he was in India he originally planned a textbook of judo for his students. The present book is a development from that original plan, enriched by his many years of sub-sequent experience and study.

There is no doubt that this book will be of great value to students of judo abroad. Mr. Harold E. Sharp, *san-dan* (3rd grade) and one of the most diligent students at the Institute at present, rendered invaluable assistance in making the book accessible to the foreign student.

With the tremendous growth of interest in judo abroad in recent years, many English textbooks of judo have made their appearance. Considering the exceptional record of the author, however, I believe this work to be the most reliable and helpful among them.

Tokyo, September 30, 1956

RISEI KANO
President,
Kodokan Judo Institute

preface

*t*he *author* of this book, Mr. Shinzo Takagaki, was born in Tokyo, Japan, in 1893. At the age of twelve he entered the Enrei-ryu Jujitsu School and studied under Mr. Yokota who was at that time the leading exponent of *jujitsu*. After four years, Mr. Takagaki transferred to the Kodokan Judo Institute, where he studied under Jigoro Kano. Within approximately a year, he obtained the grade of *ni-dan* (2nd grade); and the next year achieved *san-dan* (3rd grade). This was rapid progress, indeed, as the competitive standards were so high that advancement was difficult. During his college days Mr. Takagaki rose to *yon-dan* (4th grade), which was and is still the grade of a teacher of judo. After his graduation, he went to the United States, moving on to Canada after only six months. He studied at the University of British Columbia in Vancouver for three years, during which time he maintained his interest in judo by both practicing and teaching. The Vancouver judo *dojo* (gym) was started as a direct result of his efforts.

Demonstrations of how judo compares with other forms of self-defense such as boxing or wrestling are not generally encouraged by the practitioners of the sport, but when Mr. Takagaki was asked to stage a benefit fight for the Japan Earthquake Fund in Tacoma, Washington, he agreed to do so. His opponent was the Pacific Coast heavyweight wrestling champion, Dick Davyscot (the name may be incorrectly given). Mr. Takagaki weighed at that time 145 pounds. To make things more interesting, the bout was a free-for-all, to last until one man was knocked out or surrendered. Both men fought hard. Mr. Takagaki threw his opponent many times; by the end of the bout some of his fingernails were torn off, and his hands were bloody. The fight lasted one hour and twenty minutes and ended in a draw. Mr. Takagaki feels that this shows how well judo can stand up to any other hand-to-hand combat sport, though in general one would do better fighting in one's own specialty, under rules applying to that specialty.

When he returned to Japan, Mr. Takagaki taught judo at Nippon University, Nippon Dental University, the Diet (Parliament) guard school, and at various middle schools. He also became an official on the Committee at Kodokan.

In 1929 Rabindranath Tagore of India sent a request to Kodokan for a judo instructor for Santiniketan University. Mr. Takagaki was sent in response to this request and taught judo in India for two years. During that time he prepared the text of this book, which after many revisions has become the present manual.

After his two years in India, Mr. Takagaki was sent to Afghanistan to teach judo at their military academy. The sport became very popular with the military, and through this relationship, a Japanese embassy was established in Afghanistan. Mr. Takagaki taught for five years in Afghanistan before returning to Japan.

In 1952 Mr. Takagaki, at the invitation of the then president, Mr. Juan Peron, went to Argentina with Mr. Yoshimatsu, *shichi-dan* (7th grade), All-Japan Champion, and Mr. Osawa, *roku-dan* (6th grade). They toured Argentina, Brazil, Peru, Cuba, Mexico, and the United States.

Today Mr. Takagaki is *kyu-dan* (9th grade) and a Kodokan special instructor. In addition, he is a foreign section instructor, and chief examiner for grade-holders at Kodokan.

The authors are greatly indebted to Mr. Miyoshi Doteuchi, *san-dan* (3rd grade), of Nihon University for his wholehearted cooperation in the preparation of the illustrations for the book.

Special credit is due Mr. Cook C. Hadly, Jr., *san-dan* (3rd grade), who provided the cover photograph and a number of the tournament shots included.

HAROLD E. SHARP
3rd grade, Kodokan

contents

PART *I*

introduction

CHAPTER *1*

outline of judo

*J*udo *is both* an art and a sport, a means of defense, and equally, a means of offense. Like *jujitsu*, its forerunner, judo is a method of turning an opponent's strength against himself, thus defeating him in the most efficient manner. *Jujitsu* was practiced seriously for many years in olden days as a means of killing or seriously injuring one's opponent, but with the advent of modern warfare the need for hand-to-hand combat diminished, until the sport almost died out.

In 1882 Mr. Jigoro Kano, a student of *jujitsu*, founded the Kodokan Judo Institute in Tokyo. There he formulated a new system of bare-handed fighting which he named "judo." Judo means "the gentle way," and utilizes the very best of the *jujitsu* techniques, eliminating the harmful ones, and modifying others so that they can be practiced safely.

Judo is beneficial to both young and old, and age is no disqualification for becoming skillful. It exercises a benign effect on all the faculties of the student; and in emergencies can be used for self-defense, which of course constitutes one of the chief reasons why judo is so popular with police forces and the like.

THE OBJECTIVES

In a narrow sense judo can be defined as the study of the maximum use of the body and mind for the purposes of attack and defense. In a wider sense the principles of judo can be applied to all affairs of life. The ultimate objective of judo is the perfection of one's self by the systematic training of the mind and body through exercise so that each works in harmony with the other. Only such a person can be a valuable asset to his society.

It has been said that all games originated from some form

of actual combat which, over the years, changed into sports. Judo today maintains the martial aspect of those early games. Its objectives are as follows:

1. Development of the body
2. Skill in contest
3. Mental and moral development

These objectives cannot be considered separately, but only in close conjunction with each other. In gymnastics one simply improves the muscles by mechanical movements of the limbs, and it is quite natural that there exists neither much interest nor much benefit in it. Judo is entirely different from gymnastics in that it is intended for the harmonious development of the body by bringing all groups of muscles into play, and in that it uses the mental abilities to supplement and advance one's skill in the sport.

The judo player must always keep in mind the eventual outcome of the contest; his mind and body must work as one, always alert to the demands of the moment, his body able to move flexibly and with agility. Such automatic command of one's movement prepares the player to meet and avoid any threat. Although the proper use of the body is important, one's mental attitude is equally important for self-control and for grasping the opportunity of the moment, enabling you to defeat your opponent under adverse conditions.

The cultivation of the mind and morals naturally follows the close observance of true sportsmanship. Life is, as it were, a continuous struggle for existence, and only by applying the theory of games in personal affairs can one secure the knowledge necessary for success.

To sum up: first we must develop the body; second, we must defeat the opponent; and finally we must cultivate our morals. These are the true objectives of judo. If a student is wrong in thought or conduct he cannot be said to have mastered judo no matter how developed in body or techniques he may be.

THE TECHNIQUES

There are many different techniques in judo, but, as it is an entirely individual skill, the methods of application differ considerably among different teachers. The techniques expounded in this book are based on the more than forty years of experience of Mr. Takagaki. The following outline indicates briefly the various methods involved.

1. *Tachi-waza* (also known as *nage-waza*): standing and throwing techniques.
2. *Ne-waza* (also known as *katame-waza*): lying and grappling techniques.
3. *Atemi-waza:* striking techniques.

Tachi-waza is a method of throwing the opponent by quick and harmonious action of the body. It requires long training for good form and timing. Since there is little time to ponder during a match, one's actions must be as automatic as a reflex. Throwing techniques may be classified as follows:

1. *Te-waza:* hand throws
2. *Koshi-waza:* hip throws
3. *Ashi-waza:* foot and leg throws
4. *Sutemi-waza* (techniques of throwing the opponent by throwing yourself on the mat)
    a. *Ma-sutemi-waza:* back throws
    b. *Yoko-sutemi-waza:* side throws

Although the above classifications specify the use of a particular part of the body, all techniques require body action.

Ne-waza includes the following methods for fighting the opponent on the ground.

1. *Osaekomi-waza:* holding techniques
2. *Shime-waza:* strangling techniques
3. *Kansetsu-waza:* armlock techniques

Atemi-waza includes the methods of striking the opponent's body. Only the theory of this technique is studied, as it is never practiced today. *(See page 20.)*

THE CONTESTS

In a judo contest, only one point is needed to defeat the opponent. Because there is no second chance, both contestants are under great strain. The contest lasts only a few seconds, though it may seem like hours to the contestants. Proficiency in a contest is one of the ultimate tests of a judoman's ability. Points may be awarded on the following basis:

1. A clean throw that lands the opponent on his back.
2. Holding the opponent for thirty seconds from the moment the referee calls time on the hold. If the opponent coils his legs around one of your legs, time is not counted. You must have complete control of his body.
3. Making the opponent surrender by applying a strangling hold or by twisting the elbow joint. No part of the opponent's body may be twisted other than the elbow.

In the event that neither opponent obtains a point within the allotted time, then the referee may arbitrarily award the decision. A contestant may lose by default or by unsportsman-like behavior. Although such occurrences are rare among judo-men, the rules provide for such contingencies.

Grading in judo is based on one's ability. This ability is usually measured by proficiency in contests; but it is also judged by special examinations and by the student's general conduct as well as knowledge of judo. Differences in grading are shown by differences in the color of the belts worn with the judo suit. Beginners wear brown or white belts. Within the beginner's group there are five classes, from 5th to 1st class. The top three classes wear a brown belt. After a student is graded he wears a black belt. The grades range from 1st grade to 10th grade. Special types of belts are worn by high-grade practitioners, like the red-and-white belt from 6th through 8th grades and the red belt for 9th and 10th grades.

GRADE		COLOR OF BELT
ju-dan	10th grade	red or black
kyu-dan	9th grade	red or black
hachi-dan	8th. grade	red & white or black
shichi-dan	7th grade	red & white or black
roku-dan	6th grade	red & white or black
go-dan	5th grade	black
yon-dan	4th grade	black
san-dan	3rd grade	black
ni-dan	2nd grade	black
sho-dan	1st grade	black
ik-kyu	1st class	brown
ni-kyu	2nd class	brown
san-kyu	3rd class	brown
yon-kyu	4th class	white
go-kyu	5th class	white

PRACTICE AND TRAINING

Judo is practiced in a room called a *dojo*. The floor of the *dojo* is covered with *tatami* (straw matting). This floor is usually suspended on coil springs in order to absorb the shock of the falls. *Judo-ka* (judo-men) wear a suit called *judo-gi*. This suit consists of loose-fitting cotton trousers and a strongly woven cotton jacket. The bottom of the trousers should be halfway down the lower leg, and the sleeves of the jacket should be halfway down the forearm. The trousers are tied by means of a draw string, and the jacket is fastened by a belt which wraps around the waist twice and is tied with a square knot in the front. It is important to keep the knot of the belt in front of you at all times as it may hurt you if it is elsewhere when you fall. The following exercises comprise the normal training schedule:

1. Warming up and limbering the body
2. *Randori* (free practice)
3. *Kata* (prearranged exercises demonstrating judo principles)
4. *Uchikomi* (form practice)

Warming up and limbering the body is as necessary in judo as in any other sport requiring preparation for active participation. It also aids in developing the body. In addition to these general calisthenics special exercises are necessary. Some of these exercises are shown on pages 10–11.

Uchikomi (form practice) is a method of developing proper form by repeating the application of a technique many times. It is usually done with a partner who retains his position as you practice moving in and out, applying a technique. At first the form is practiced without actually throwing the partner. Next one should attempt to throw the partner on every tenth try. By working assiduously, one will become so proficient that one will not have to think of form, and will be able to apply automatically the correct technique for any opening.

Some students think that judo is only a matter of learning a few tricks which can then be applied for self-defense or physical culture. They may be enthusiastic at the beginning, but when they find they cannot make as much progress in a short time as they had expected they drop out. But as in all other activities, there are grades of skill in judo. Slow and steady progress will take the student where he wants to go. Practice in judo goes on continuously for many years, and it is possible to keep on learning, no matter how long one studies.

It is erroneous to think that judo is only for the mature young man. There can be found in judo a curriculum suitable to both the very young whose bodies are not yet developed, and for the elderly who wish to retain their flexibility. With proper practice the old will become healthier and the weak will become stronger. They will learn how the weaker can master techniques to overcome the stronger. Naturally, those who begin young will have an advantage, but that does not mean that older persons cannot profit. The best ages to begin judo are between eleven and thirty. The better mentally equipped a student is, the better he can study judo.

It is essential in daily practice to apply the proper techniques at the proper time. It is also important to train our minds as well. Even those who can perform well in practice often lose in a contest because they cannot control themselves under the demand of circumstances. Fear, anxiety, and irritation at an opponent may act to keep one from seeing an opening or to waste one's strength at random. If an opponent seems dull, one is likely to underestimate him, thus leaving oneself off guard and liable to an unexpected defeat. This is due to an undisciplined mind. Therefore, a student of judo must train his mind as well as his body in order to be in full command of all his faculties at the necessary moments.

In feudal Japan, a famous master of fencing, Miyamoto Musashi, used to say, "If the mind is as clear as a mirror, there is no need for a sword." Musashi was sitting on a bench one summer evening, without his sword, meditating. One of his pupils surprised him by coming from behind him with a dagger in his hand to test his master's skill. Musashi calmly stepped back, pulling an end of the mat which covered the bench. The disciple fell headlong, at which Musashi said, "What are you doing?" Thus, if we discipline our minds and keep them clear as a mirror, we will be sure to have the necessary resourcefulness and presence of mind to deal with any situation, no matter how alarming it might be.

CHAPTER 2
preliminaries

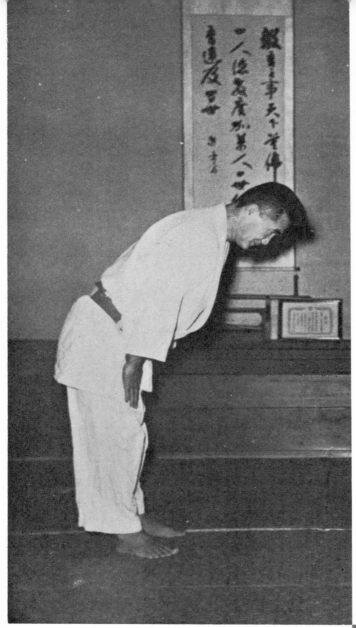

rei: salutations

Figures 1-6 *(bowing from a kneeling position)*. Kneel on the mat and sit upright with your buttocks resting on your feet and your hands on your thighs. Place your hands on the mat before you and bow with your head approximately one foot from the mat. Return to the first position, sitting upright. To stand, rise on your knees and toes, then step forward with your right foot and finally stand up in a natural position.

Facing page *(bowing from a standing position)*. Face your opponent and stand erect in a natural position. Bow, bending forward approximately 45 degrees, and, placing your hands on your thighs, rise and resume the natural position.

taiso: calisthenics

Before practice it is necessary to exercise in order to limber and warm-up your body. General calisthenics are satisfactory. The illustrations on this page show some exercises which are especially appropriate for judo.

shizen-tai, jigo-tai: postures

Figures 1-3 (*shizen-tai:* natural posture). It is necessary always to stand in a natural position, keeping your mind alert. From this position you can move freely and can, as the circumstances may require, attack your opponent or defend yourself. In the natural position you stand with both feet slightly apart, your body straight, and your weight slightly on the balls of your feet. Your legs should not be stiff but slightly flexed with the knees bent diagonally forward and outward. If your knees are bent straight forward, you can be easily unbalanced toward your front. From the natural position you can shift your weight quickly to either leg when the opponent attacks, and can avoid being thrown. If you stiffen your body against the opponent's attack, it will be difficult to move and you will be easily defeated. Therefore, the importance of maintaining a free natural position cannot be overemphasized.

Figures 4-6 (*jigo-tai:* defensive posture). A defensive posture is assumed by spreading your legs wide apart and bending your knees to lower your body. This position makes it difficult for the opponent to attack you. At the same time, however, it makes it difficult for you to attack the opponent or to escape his attack. This position has its definite use at the right time. You must use whichever position is best according to the circumstances when fighting. Do not try to remain in any fixed position but continue to move, changing your position in order to maintain your balance.

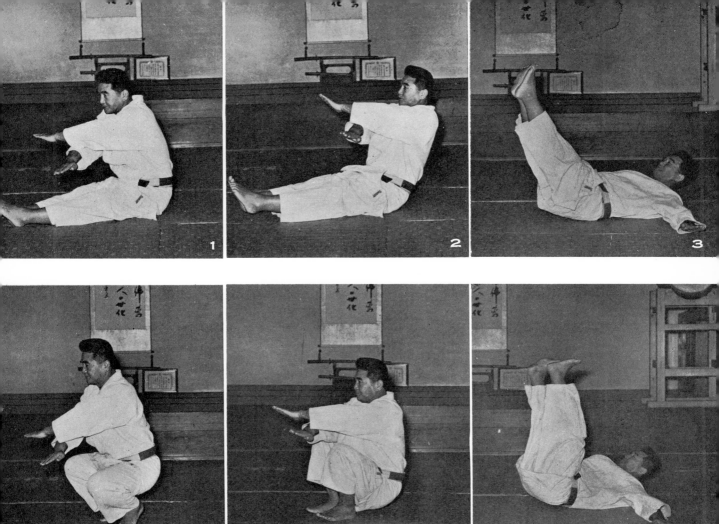

ukemi: falling exercises

Falling properly is one of the most important phases of judo and cannot be overestimated. The purpose of falling exercises is to learn to control your body when thrown and to break the shock of the fall. Learning to fall is quite simple and is the first lesson in judo. Falling exercises are also done for warming-up before the regular training schedule.

Figures 1-3 (falling backward from a sitting position). From a sitting position, start by crossing your arms out in front of you, keeping your chin tucked in, then fall backward. As you fall slap the mat with both of your arms, striking it with the forearm and hand. It is important to be relaxed and to keep your chin tucked in to prevent striking your head against the mat.

Figures 4-6 (falling backward from a squatting position). Squat low, crossing your arms in front of you, and fall backward, keeping your chin tucked in and slap the mat hard as you fall.

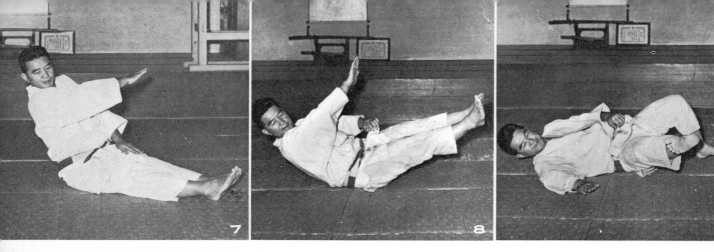

Figures 7-9 (falling sideways from a sitting position). From a sitting position, raise your right arm out in front and across your body. Fall back, rolling your body to the right. As you fall keep your chin tucked in, looking down toward your right foot. Slap the mat hard as you fall and let your feet down on the mat as shown in Figure 9. It is important that your feet do not touch each other when falling sideways, as the bones striking each other may cause injury. Now quickly roll your body to the left and slap the mat, assuming the same position as before. Continue to practice rolling from one side to the other.

Figures 10-12 (falling sideways from a squatting position). From a squatting position, raise your right arm out in front and across your body and step out with your right foot. You will now lose your balance and naturally fall to your right side. Slap the mat hard as you fall, keeping your chin tucked in. Resume the squatting position and practice falling to the left, reversing the above directions. The sideways fall is the most important method of falling in judo.

Figures 13-15 (*tumbling forward from a crouched position*). With your right foot forward, bend your body low, touching the mat with your hands. Point the fingers of your right hand inward and the fingers of the left hand forward. Now with a slight push with your feet roll forward. Keep your chin tucked in and curve your right hand in deeply as you roll. This prevents your head and right shoulder from striking the mat. As you land on your back, slap the mat with your left arm and break the fall. Resume the standing position and practice tumbling with your left foot forward, reversing the above directions.

Figures 16-19 (*tumbling forward from a standing position*). Step forward with your right foot, raising your right hand in front of you and curving the fingers inward. Tumble forward, keeping your chin tucked in, touching lightly the mat with both hands. Keep your arms flexible and relaxed as you tumble; do not straighten your arms. As you land on your back, slap the mat hard with your left hand. Resume the standing position and tumble forward, stepping out with the left foot, reversing the above directions.

kumikata: methods of holding

Grip the opponent's jacket firmly, keeping your arms bent and relaxed. Holding the opponent properly is extremely important as your arms will convey his movements to you, and, if your hold is poor, your arms will convey your movements to him. It is difficult to say just how tightly you should hold the opponent, for each person is different and must find his own method of working. Control the opponent's body with the movement of your own body, and not by pushing or pulling with your arms. This will enable you to keep your arms in a flexed position at all times. There are various methods of holding the opponent as are shown in the following illustrations:

Figures 1–2. From the right natural position grip the outside of his right elbow with your left hand and his left lapel with your right hand. Generally this is the best position for controlling the opponent and applying throwing techniques to throw him to his right side.

Figure 3. Grip your opponent's right sleeve near the shoulder with your left hand and his left lapel with your right hand. This grip is similar to that in Figures 1–2, except for the left hand. This method is useful when applying shoulder throws such as *ippon-seoi-nage.*

Figure 4. Grip both sleeves near the shoulders. This method is useful when applying throws to either the right or the left.

Figure 5. Grip the opponent's sleeves behind the elbows. This method is good for applying foot sweeping techniques, counter-techniques, or *sode-tsurikomi-goshi*.

Figures 6-7. Grip the opponent's right sleeve behind the elbow with your left hand and with your right reach under his left armpit and grip the back of his jacket. This method is useful in unbalancing the opponent to his right front corner and in applying a technique such as *harai-gosh*

Figure 8. Grip the opponent's right sleeve at the elbow with your left hand and the back of his left collar with your right hand. This is a very strong method to use in breaking the opponent's balance forward when applying techniques such as *uchi-mata* or *hane-goshi*.

kuzushi: methods of unbalancing the opponent

Unbalancing the opponent is one of the most important actions in judo. When the opponent is unbalanced he is weak in relation to you, and you can easily control his body. It is extremely difficult to throw your opponent if he is not first unbalanced. Most beginners in judo make the mistake of trying to apply a technique without first unbalancing their opponents and for this reason they are not successful.

There are eight directions in which a standing person can be unbalanced.

Figure 1. Pushing him back on his heels.

Figures 2 & 8. Pushing him diagonally backward when he stands with his weight on his backward foot.

Figures 3 & 7. Pulling him sideways, bringing his weight to the outer edge of one foot.

Figures 4 & 6. Pulling him diagonally forward when he stands with his weight on his forward foot.

Figure 5. Pulling him up and forward on his toes.

We have just discussed unbalancing an opponent when he is stationary; however, he can also be unbalanced as he moves about by proper timing. For instance, when the opponent steps forward with his right foot he must temporarily rest his weight on the left foot. After his right foot touches the ground, it will bear his weight and be difficult to move. Therefore, just as the right foot is about to touch the ground, sweep it out from under him with your foot. His foot is similar to a heavy stone hanging from the end of a rope which is easily moved while off the ground, but is impossible to budge when resting on the ground. As an opponent moves to and fro he is constantly shifting his weight, offering easy chances for you to attack if you are alert.

In addition to unbalancing the opponent's body it is also important to try to unbalance his mind. This can be best done by maintaining your own relaxed state of mind. Your superior mental posture will cause a feeling of uncertainty and weakness in your opponent. If you can accomplish this, then more than half of the battle is won. Sometimes tricks such as shouting, slapping some part of your body, creating a sharp sound, or a jerk will startle the opponent.

1

2

8

3

7

6

5

4

atemi-waza: striking techniques

The illustrations on this page show some of the various methods
of striking the opponent. These techniques are practiced without
actually striking the partner with whom you practice. In order
to develop striking power a padded board is usually used.
Although this phase of judo is very interesting it is never used
in judo matches and is only demonstrated as a possible means
of self-defense.

PART II
tachi-waza:
throwing techniques

CHAPTER 3
te-waza: hand throws

*i*n *judo* there are three distinct elements involved in accomplishing a *tachi-waza*, a throw from a standing position. The first is *kuzushi*, or unbalancing the opponent, which has already been discussed. The second is *tsukuri*, or the movements and positions that have to be taken to set up yourself and the opponent for the throw, and the third is the actual throw itself.

In this and the following three chapters various throwing techniques, escapes, and counter-throws will be described. In each case the techniques are described for throwing the opponent to his right, whether forward or backward. Any of these techniques may be applied from the left by reversing the directions. The authors have tried to present the "why" and "how" of each technique so that the student will understand the basic principles of the throws and will not perform mechanical motions. Emphasis is constantly placed on the principle of balance and minimum effort. Unbalancing the opponent first and placing yourself in a proper position before applying a throw are of utmost importance. If you succeed in doing so the actual throw itself should require relatively little effort.

Tachi-waza are classified as follows, according to the part of the body which is most essential in accomplishing a throw.

1. *Te-waza:* hand throws
2. *Koshi-waza:* hip throws
3. *Ashi-waza:* leg throws
4. *Sutemi-waza:* back and side throws

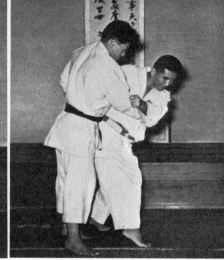

tai-otoshi: forward body drop

In this technique you unbalance the opponent to his right front corner by lifting him up on his toes as he moves forward. He can also be thrown sideways and when he moves backward, but this is more difficult. The opponent is thrown in a large circular motion across your right leg. The thrust of your hands is the essential factor in this technique.

Figures 1-4. As the opponent steps forward with his right foot, drop down, stepping back with your left foot and pivoting on your right foot. Simultaneously, pull the opponent forward and push upward with your hands, making him come up on his toes. Quickly cut your right foot across the front of the opponent's right foot. Throw by pivoting to your left, pulling him down hard in a circular motion, and snapping his leg up by coming up on your right toes. The pull of your hands is most important. Turn your head to the left, which directs your body in that direction and aids the forward pull of your arms. Sometimes the opponent is made to come forward by first pushing him back, and the technique is then applied just as his right foot moves forward to counter your push.

Figures 5-7. As the opponent takes a step forward with his right foot, turn and step in the direction of his motion with your left foot, your toes pointing in the same direction as his. Simultaneously, pull him forward and up with your hands, making his balance come to the ball of his right foot. Next, step across his right foot with your right and apply the technique.

Figures 8-10. When the opponent moves sideways to his right, step in that direction with your left foot, your toes pointing in the same direction. Simultaneously lift him up to his front and to his right. Quickly step across his right leg, pulling your left elbow in hard toward your stomach and pushing up with your right hand, as if turning a wheel.

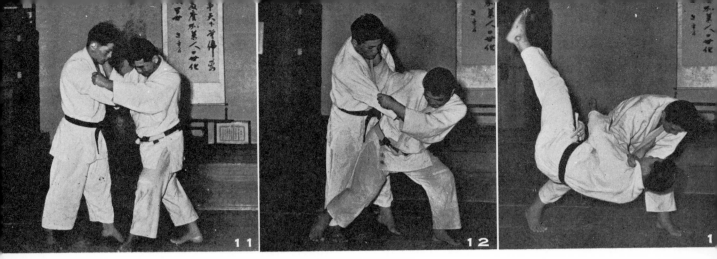

Figures 11-13. As the opponent steps back with his right foot, jump low into position, with your right foot following his right as it moves back. Just as his right foot comes to rest you are underneath him and your arms are pushing him up and forward. This application requires exceptional timing and speed. If *tai-otoshi* fails and the opponent pulls back, *o-uchi-gari* (Figure 14, see also page 61) may be applied by sweeping his left foot with your right.

COUNTER-TECHNIQUES

Tai-otoshi is generally applied by the opponent standing on one leg, say his left, bringing his right leg across to the front of your right foot, and pulling you down across his right leg. If you are trained in judo, you will sense the technique as he turns and places his right foot across your right. His balance then is weak toward his front and back. So, if you step forward behind his left heel with your right foot and press down diagonally toward his left, you will be in a strong position, and his weight will rest on his left heel. Further pressure will make his position weak and prevent him from applying the move. He can be thown down on his back by pulling backward and pressing down heavily. If you do not wish to throw him on his back, you may apply an armlock as shown in Figures 15–17.

Another method of stopping the opponent is to bend your knees and press the right knee down behind the back of his right knee. As the opponent is dependent upon the abrupt upward thrust of his right leg for executing the throw, your pressure on the back of his right leg will stop him.

A method of counter-throwing the opponent is shown in Figures 18–21. As previously explained, the opponent is weak toward his front. Push forward and step over his right leg with your right foot, touching the mat at the opponent's center of gravity. Lift your left foot out of the way and push down with your left hand and pull his left arm hard with your right hand. This will throw him in a big circular motion to his left.

24 : tachi-waza

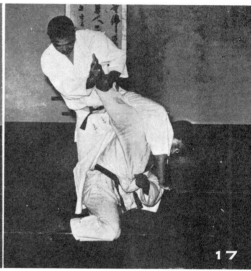

te-waza : 25

ippon-seoi-nage: one arm shoulder throw

The principle of this technique is to place your back under the opponent's center of gravity and to throw him straight over your shoulder so that he lands in front of you. The hold for this technique is a slight variation on the standard hold. Your left hand grips the opponent's arm at his right shoulder instead of at his elbow for a stronger pull.

Figures 1-4. As you and the opponent move about the mat, watch for the time he is in the natural position. If he is stiff, you might push him backward first so that he will come forward more easily. Then pull him up and toward you, bringing his weight up on his toes. Still pulling strongly with your left hand, bring your right arm under his right armpit, hooking his upper arm tightly in the bend of your arm. Drive up hard with your shoulders as you hook his arm. This will add force in bringing him up on his toes. At the same time bring your right foot to the front of the opponent's right, stepping on the ball of your foot so that you can turn freely. Pivoting on your right foot, bring your left foot back in front of his left, turning your body in a counterclockwise motion. Now your feet should be parallel, knees well bent, with the opponent up on his toes tightly against your back. Throw him over your shoulder in the direction of his right shoulder in a semicircle by springing up with your hip and pulling down hard with your arms. It is essential that you keep pulling forward strongly at all times in order to prevent the opponent from dropping down to a strong natural position. In this technique you turn your back toward the opponent with your weight on one leg. This puts you in a dangerously weak position. It is, therefore, extremely important to first unbalance the opponent and to keep him unbalanced until the throw is completed.

26 : tachi-waza

Figures 5-6. Another way is to lead the opponent forward. As his right foot advances and your left retreats, pull strongly with your left arm, making his weight come to his right toe. Now, continuing the pull, bring your right foot between his feet and pivot counterclockwise on the ball of your right foot. This should bring your feet parallel to each other and directly under the opponent. The knees should be well bent. At the time of the turn, hook his right arm hard and follow through with the throw as previously described. The power of your hip springing up against the opponent's right abdomen adds considerable power to the throw. Keep turning counterclockwise with your hip shifted slightly to the right in order to prevent the opponent from escaping in that direction.

Sometimes you may encounter an opponent who is stiff-armed and prevents you from coming in close. As the opponent straightens his arms to push you away, release the grip of your right hand. Take a step back with your left foot, pulling with your left hand. Suddenly, press down on the opponent's left hand with your right arm, clamping it tightly under the armpit. Now his left arm is immobilized and your right shoulder should be low. Keeping this grip, quickly enter inside by turning on your right foot and bring your left foot back, touching the right side of his lower abdomen with your right hip. Grip his right arm with both of your arms as originally described and throw him. Throughout this move, his left hand will be clamped under your right arm.

Figures 7–8. If the opponent resists when you apply this technique, quickly drop down on your right knee, then throw him. In this position you are lower than the opponent and the sudden drop of your body adds power to your pull. Your right leg is alongside his right leg, preventing him from escaping in that direction.

Uchi-makikomi may also be applied if the opponent resists.

COUNTER-TECHNIQUES

Counter-techniques for *ippon-seoi-nage* and *seoi-nage* are quite similar since the weaknesses in the opponent's position when applying either technique are the same. The opponent's greatest weakness is toward his rear. Therefore, you must shift your weight to your left rear in order to counter the force of the throw.

Figures 9 & 10. As the opponent applies the technique, quickly jump around to the left side and pull him down or, when the opponent applies *ippon-seoi-nage*, step back with your left foot, pulling him backward. Then apply a choke hold such as *okuri-eri-jime*.

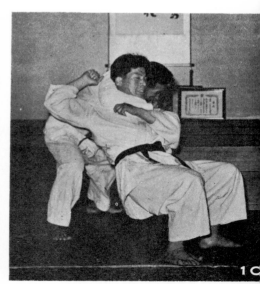

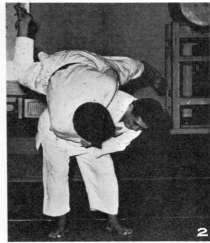

seoi-nage: shoulder throw

This technique is properly called *morote-seoi-nage* (two-arm shoulder throw); however, *seoi-nage* is the commonly used term. The principle of this technique is the same as in *ippon-seoi-nage* except for the use of your right arm.

Figures 1-2. Grip the opponent's jacket in the normal manner. If the opponent is strong and pushes you backward, allow him to do so, but at the same time give him a stronger pull so that he may take a longer step forward than he expected. Take one step back with your left foot, keeping balance on your right. Turn your body counterclockwise, your left foot circumscribing a circle on the mat as you step back under the opponent. Keep the opponent pulled well forward with your left hand and bring your right forearm under his right armpit. Pull hard so that his chest is tightly against your back, with your hip slightly to the right and knees well bent. Throw by snapping up hard with your hips and pulling down violently with your arms, coming up on your toes.

Figure 3. If the opponent attempts to escape the move by stepping to his left side, pull down hard, dropping to your right knee.

Figure 4. If you lose your grip with the left hand as the opponent attempts to avoid the move, drop down to your right knee. Then reach up with your left hand and grip high on the opponent's right lapel. Throw with a violent pull.

Figures 5-6. This technique is best applied when the opponent is in a defensive stance or when his right leg is pulled back. In the latter case, catch the opponent as he steps back with his right leg. Apply the throw quickly by pivoting to the left on your left foot and dropping low across his right leg with your right leg. This action will block his right leg and bring his body against your back. As you drop down pull the opponent forward with your arms and turn your right forearm under his right armpit. Throw the opponent over your right hip by pulling down with your arms and springing up with your right leg.

Figure 7. Following is another form of *seoi-nage* which is applied when the opponent pushes you. From the standard standing position, pivot clockwise on your right foot and drop down to your left knee directly in front of the opponent. As you pull hard, the opponent's waist should rest across the back of your left shoulder. Throw the opponent over your shoulder by pulling with the right hand and pushing his left leg up with the back of your left hand. This technique may be applied without touching the ground with your knee. You can squat low and pivot clockwise.

Seoi-nage may be applied in conjunction with techniques such as *harai-goshi* or *uchi-mata*. When any of these throws are applied the opponent is raised up and forward. At this point you can turn your right forearm under him and apply *seoi-nage*.

COUNTER-TECHNIQUES

Counter-techniques for *ippon-seoi-nage* and *seoi-nage* are fairly similar, since the same weaknesses exist in the opponent's position when applying either technique. The opponent's greatest weakness is to his rear. Therefore, you must shift your weight to the left rear in order to counter the force of the throw.

Figure 8. As the opponent applies *seoi-nage*, step back with your left foot and press down on his right shoulder with both hands.

Figures 9-10. Avoid the move by bending your knees forward. Then, grasping the opponent's right arm firmly against your chest, bring your left leg against the right side of his neck and apply pressure to the elbow.

kata-guruma: shoulder wheel throw

The principle of this technique is to drop low, pulling the opponent across the back of your shoulder, and then to throw by standing up and pulling him over your shoulder. This is a violent throw as it drops the opponent from the standing height of your shoulders.

Figures 1-4. As the opponent steps forward on his right foot or stands with his feet wide apart, pull his right arm forward. It may be best to grip his right sleeve high by the shoulder for better leverage. As his weight comes forward to his right foot, step in with your right foot and bend your knees deeply with your legs apart for balance. Pulling continuously, move your body in such a way that your right shoulder touches his right hip. Now, catch his right thigh with your right arm, and applying shoulder force lift him up on your shoulders. Throw by standing up on your toes, lifting his legs with your right hand and pulling him violently over the shoulders with the left hand.

Another method is used when the opponent steps to his left side. At that time pull hard with your left hand, dropping to the mat on your left knee. Pulling him over your shoulders, spring up and throw as described above.

COUNTER-TECHNIQUES

As the opponent brings his head against your stomach, press down hard on his neck, encircling his head with your right arm. From this position you can apply a choke hold or merely prevent him from applying the technique.

Figures 5-9. To counter-throw, bring your weight down on the opponent's back as he enters in low, touching your pelvis with his shoulder. This weakens his position to the front. Then, reaching around his body from both sides, catch his belt with both hands. Step in between his legs with your right foot, dropping to the mat on your back and throwing him with *tawara-gaeshi* as you roll over on your back.

yama-arashi: mountain storm throw

This technique is applied by gripping one side of the opponent with both hands, turning, and sweeping his supporting leg.

Pull the opponent forward, then transfer your right hand over to his right lapel, gripping deep near the neck. Pivoting on your left foot, place your right leg to the right of his right leg. As you pull hard, his right ribs should touch your ribs.

Concentrating all your force in your upper body, turn, sweeping up with your leg, and pull violently with your arms. He should land in front of your right foot.

If it is inconvenient for you to change hands, you may start by gripping his right lapel with your right hand. If he resists, bring your right forearm deep under his right armpit. When the opponent stands with his right foot drawn back, you will have to step in quickly in order to bring his body close to you.

If this move is unsuccessful, then *seoi-nage, makikomi, yoko-gakae,* or *tai-otoshi* may be applied.

COUNTER-TECHNIQUES

When the move is applied, grip the opponent's left thigh with your left hand and hook your left leg around his left leg. If the opponent falls and takes you to the ground, retain your position and try to remain on top of him so that he cannot throw you on your back.

ganseki-otoshi: stone drop

Ganseki-otoshi is rarely applied in modern practice. In ancient times it was practiced by samurai. One of the best methods to prevent a samurai from using his sword was to bind his arms from behind so that he could not draw his sword. *Ganseki-otoshi* was devised against such an attack from the rear when the opponent reaches around you from behind.

When the opponent reaches around you, spread your elbows sideways to create a space. If he locks his hands in front of you, snap your elbows sideways with force. Instantly drop down on your right knee, with the right foot between his legs. Grip his right shoulder with your right hand and right sleeve with your left hand. This will make the opponent lean forward against your back. Throw him over your right shoulder using your shoulder power. If the opponent resists, then place the back of your left hand under his left knee. Now throw him by pushing up against his left knee with your left hand and pulling his shoulder with your right hand. Counter-techniques are to pull back or to apply a choke hold.

uki-otoshi: floating drop

This technique is usually applied to the opponent's front right corner or right side and is primarily dependent on your arm power.

Figures 1-2. From the right natural position lead the opponent forward step by step, pulling him forward. As he follows with his right foot leading, take a large step backward with your left foot and at the same time drop down on your right knee, pulling strongly. This weakens his position as he will stumble forward on his right foot. At this moment throw him with a circular motion of your hands.

Figures 3-4. A good moment to apply *uki-otoshi* is when the opponent side-steps to his right. At this moment turn your body counterclockwise, your left toes following the direction of his movement. His weight will now rest on the small toes of his right foot. Now, throw him sideways with a strong lifting semicircular motion. You should bend your knees slightly and keep your abdomen pressed forward. The power for the throw comes from your arms, loins, and knees.

COUNTER-TECHNIQUES

As the opponent drops to his knee, take a big step forward with your right foot, pushing him in the direction of his own pull. Simultaneously, reach around his neck with your left hand and press him down with shoulder power. Step to his right foot and shift your weight to your left foot; twisting your body to the left, throw him down to his left rear corner.

CHAPTER *4*

koshi-waza : hip throws

tsurikomi-goshi: lifting hip throw

In this move you must bring the opponent into a weak position by pulling him forward and lifting him up on his toes. You then turn, dropping low and throwing the opponent over your right hip.

Figures 1-3. From the right natural position, pull the opponent's left shoulder forward with your right hand, making his left leg advance. At the same time slide your right foot in front of his right foot. Now, as you push up with your right arm and pull across your chest with the left arm, the opponent will be brought up and forward. Simultaneously bend low, turning your body around, pivoting on the right foot. Maintaining a low position, bend your hip to the right bringing the opponent's abdomen tightly against the back of your right hip. Throw by pulling down hard with your hands and springing up with your knees.

COUNTER-TECHNIQUES

Avoid the move by pushing the opponent forward and down as he turns into you. Try to keep your arms bent as you practice, for if they are straight he can easily apply the move. If the opponent is in a good position, drop down, bending your knees forward. Shifting your weight to your left leg will prevent you from being thrown to your right front corner. Counter-throws for this technique are similar to those for *harai-goshi*, such as *utsuri-goshi* and *ushiro-goshi*.

Figures 4-7. Another method called *sode-tsurikomi-goshi* (lifting sleeve hip throw) is applied by grasping both of the opponent's sleeves near the elbow. Pull his arms up and forward, making him come up on his toes. Stepping into position, push the opponent's left arm straight up and pull his right arm tightly across your chest. Except for the use of the opponent's sleeve

the application is the same as in *tsurikomi-goshi*. It is important to keep the opponent's left arm stretched upward at all times. If the opponent is strong and resists, pull him forward hard a few times, then, as he pulls back, take half a step forward toward him. At the same time lift his left arm up and apply the technique. Sometimes the opponent will keep his arms in close to his body. In such a case take one step forward with your right foot and rest your right elbow on your right hip. Suddenly, with the power of your hip behind the elbow, push up the opponent's left arm.

harai-goshi: sweeping loin throw

In this move, the main feature is the use of your right leg and hip. The opponent's weakness lies to his right front corner.

Figures 1-2. From the right natural posture, pull the opponent forward, with his right foot leading. As his weight comes to his right toes, slide your left foot across in front of the opponent's left foot. Suddenly and strongly pull his body against yours, pivoting counterclockwise on your left foot. The opponent's chest should be held tightly against the right rear side of your chest. Now, still pivoting to the front, sweep your right leg back, striking the opponent's lower leg with the calf of your leg. Turn your right foot and leg inward as you sweep. The sweeping of your leg and the pull of your arms will throw the opponent. For a successful application of *harai-goshi* it is absolutely necessary that the opponent be unbalanced to the extent that releasing your hold on him would cause him to fall involuntarily.

Figures 3-5. A variation is used when the opponent steps back with his right foot. At this time step forward with your left foot. Then with a sudden jerk pull forward with your arms and apply the technique, pivoting on your left foot.

Another opportunity to use this technique occurs when the opponent steps sideways to his right side. As he does so slide your left foot in front of his left foot. Apply the move immediately as originally described.

Figures 6-8. In the above method you stepped across to the opponent's left with your left foot, then executed a large pivoting motion. The following method has less movement and is applied as the opponent steps forward on his right foot. At this moment, pulling him forward, step back behind your right heel with your left foot. Then, pivoting on the left foot, pull the opponent tightly against your body and sweep with your right leg.

Figures 9-10. If you cannot throw the opponent as you sweep your leg back, then apply *harai-makikomi.* This is done by releasing your right hand and bringing it in a large circular motion over the opponent's right shoulder or alongside his head, pointing down toward the mat. Roll your body hard, counterclockwise, falling to the ground as you sweep back with your leg.

hane-goshi: springing hip throw

This move may be applied in three ways; when the opponent stands with his weight on either his forward or backward foot, or when he leans forward on both toes. In this move it is the hip power that is brought into play. If the balance of your opponent is on the center or lower part of his body, it will be difficult to lift him with your hip and leg power. You must shift his balance to the upper part of his body by pulling him toward his front.

Figures 1-3. Push the opponent's right shoulder backward; this will make him step back with his right foot. At the same time step forward with your left foot and quickly pivot on it counterclockwise, pulling his chest tightly against your right rear side. Your right hip should touch his lower abdomen. With your right leg bent, spring up against the inside of his right leg, lifting the opponent up with the power of the side of your hip and thigh. It is important that you strike his body first with the hip, using the leg only as a guide for controlling his body. In lifting the opponent keep your body turned so that it lies sideways in line with your right leg. Pulling hard, turn your body and throw him down.

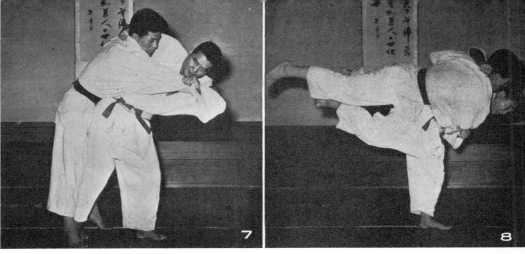

Figures 4-6. As the opponent steps forward with his right foot, step back with your left foot, bringing it behind your right. Quickly pull his body into yours, pivoting on your left foot and striking his abdomen with your right hip. Pulling constantly, turn your body and bring your right elbow into his left armpit. Bending your left knee deeply, lift his body up and throw him.

Figures 7-8. Another method is to bring the opponent's weight forward and up on his toes. This will shift his center of gravity up and to his front thus breaking his balance. If the opponent stands in a strong natural position or in a defensive position, quickly pull his body forward with force. Simultaneously skip into position, left knee well bent, and strike the opponent hard and low with your hip. It is important to keep his body held tightly against your body. When you strike his right calf-muscles with your own leg, the opponent's leg will leave the ground. Roll your body to the left as you throw, keeping a tight grip on the opponent.

Figures 9-10. If the opponent offers too much resistance, then apply *hane-makikomi*. In this move, you release your right hand, bringing it over and across the front of the opponent's head. With the fingers extended and arm curved, roll your body hard to the left, dropping to the ground with the opponent. It is not always necessary to fall to the ground, although it is the most natural thing to do in completing this throw.

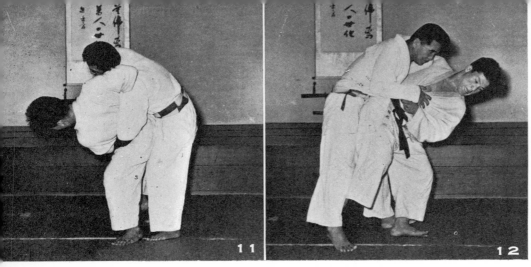

11   12

COUNTER-TECHNIQUES

Hane-goshi is applied by the opponent's bringing his right hip close to your front loin, pulling you by your right hand, and lifting you up with his hip and leg power. Your right leg is swept by his right leg. When he applies the move he stands on his left leg and is weak toward his left side. The escape is accomplished by taking advantage of his weakness.

Figures 11-12. Just as he springs into you, grip his left front thigh from the back with your left hand. Using the weight of your body, press hard to his left side. If he is strong he may still throw you with his hip power. But if you are close to the left side of his body he cannot lift you. Now, you may still find it difficult to escape as he is still pulling you forward with his left hand. Hence, still pressing toward his left side, pull your right hand loose from his grip and turn your body slightly to the right, so that his hip cannot be applied against your right loin. If he still applies *hane-makikomi*, falling to the ground, you can escape if you already have lifted your right leg; so that when he falls over, you can bring your right leg forward and support yourself. This method of escaping is also applicable in avoiding other moves such as *harai-goshi*, *uchi-mata*, *tsurikomi-goshi*, etc.

Figures 13-15. As the opponent applies this move, shift your weight to your left, stopping his throw. Then, as the opponent starts to recover his position, pull quickly with your right hand and push with your left. Simultaneously, sweep his left supporting leg out from under him with the sole of your right foot. This technique is called *sasae-tsurikomi-ashi-harai* and is described later in the book.

13   14   15

Figures 16-17. Another counter-throw is to apply *ura-nage.* In this move the opponent is raised off the ground and thrown backward to your left side as you fall with him.

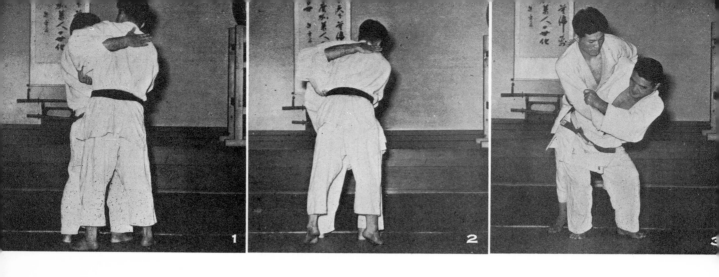

uki-goshi: floating hip throw

This move can be applied directly as a means of attack or as a counter-throw for defense. To apply the move directly, release your right hand grip as the opponent moves to your right and slide your right arm deep under his left armpit and around his back. At the same time turn your back into the opponent, pushing your right hip across the right side of his front hip. Pulling hard with your left arm and keeping the opponent's body pulled forward and against your body, throw him over your right hip by giving your body a hard counterclockwise twist.

Uki-goshi can also be used as a counter-throw after you have stopped the action of the opponent when he attempts to throw you forward. In this case quickly step in front of the opponent, slipping an arm around his back, and throw him over your hip with a twisting motion.

Ushiro-goshi or *utsuri-goshi* can be easily applied as counter-techniques.

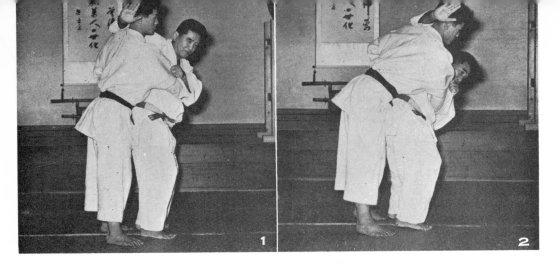

kubi-nage: neck throw

Controlling the opponent's body is very important in this move. Grip the opponent's right sleeve tightly, pulling his arm across your chest. Step forward and in front of his right foot, catching his head tightly in the bend of your right arm. Then step back with your left foot, putting your hips into his abdomen. If the opponent is stiff he can easily be thrown over your right hip, but if he is relaxed it will be difficult. As you pull forward on his neck he will rear back and stiffen. At this time drop down, bending your knees, then throw him by snapping your hip upward, straightening the knees and pulling with your arms. Also twist your body counterclockwise to the left as you throw him.

koshi-nage: hip throw

As the opponent steps back with his right foot, take a large step forward with your right foot, across and behind his right. Quickly turn and lower your body, pivoting on your toes and bending your left knee deep at a 90 degree angle. Your left elbow should touch your left thigh as you pull, and the right forearm should be brought under the opponent's left armpit. Throw by a pulling and twisting motion over your right hip.

o-goshi: major hip throw

This is a basic hip throw. It is similar to *tsurikomi-goshi*, *uki-goshi*, etc., except for the position of your right arm. Pulling with your left arm and turning your body into the opponent, bring your right forearm deep under his left armpit. You may grip his left lapel or the sleeve near the left armpit with your right hand. Keeping the opponent's body held tightly against your right rear side, with his balance to his right front corner, throw by springing up with your hips, turning in a counterclockwise direction.

obi-otoshi: belt lifting drop

This technique is difficult to apply on an alert opponent. However, if the opponent is inattentive or in a weak position it can be applied. Grip the opponent's front belt with your right hand and pull him forward while stepping back and around with your right foot. As the opponent resists and pulls backward, step around behind him, placing your left foot behind his left foot, and bend low. Quickly raise the opponent by pulling with your right hand and by snapping your abdomen forward against his buttocks. Your left hand is also behind his hip pushing up to raise his body. Throw the opponent on his back along your left side. Sometimes it may be necessary to throw yourself in order to throw a strong opponent.

1

2

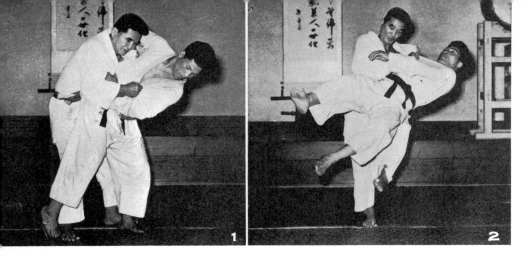

ushiro-goshi: rear hip throw

This move is applied primarily as a counter-throw against the opponent when he applies any technique which makes him turn his back into the front of your body. You can apply *ushiro-goshi* directly by stepping behind your opponent, but this is not practical in actual use.

Figures 1-2. As the opponent applies a move such as *harai-goshi*, quickly bend your knees forward and slide your left hand around his waist to prevent the opponent's throw. Then quickly snap your abdomen up and forward forcing the opponent's body up in the air. Next, step back and, using your right hand as a guide, drive the opponent's back into the mat. As shown in the illustrations you may use your left knee under his buttocks in order to raise his body forward.

Figures 3-4. Another method of applying this technique is to grip the opponent's left leg above the knee with your left hand and to step around his left rear side. Still gripping his left leg, bend forward around his left side and bring your right arm across the front of his body, gripping his belt as far to the right as possible. Now, snap your abdomen forward against his buttocks, pulling up at the same time with your left hand and pushing his upper body back with your right arm and shoulder. The opponent's body will then be lifted horizontally. Then throw him on his back at your right side.

utsuri-goshi: switching hip throw

This is primarily a counter-technique like *ushiro-goshi* and is used when the opponent attempts to throw you forward, usually with a hip technique.

Let us say that the opponent attempts to apply *hane-goshi*. Suddenly reach around his waist with your left hand and bend your knees so that your loin is back a little. Now, lift him up with force, using the thrust of your abdomen and hands as in *ushiro-goshi*. While you are lifting him up a little space is created between your bodies. At that moment, quickly turn your left hip forward so that his body now rests across your hip. As he touches your left hip spring up with your knees, throwing him over your hip. It is necessary to pull his left hand hard with your right and to turn your hip clockwise when throwing the opponent. If the opponent does not come across your left hip when you turn and remains on his left foot, then spring your left leg against his leg as in *hane-goshi* or *harai-goshi*. Sometimes the opponent will wind his legs about yours to prevent being thrown. In this case take a few steps back and apply *ura-nage* or *ushiro-goshi*.

counter-techniques for koshi-waza

Generally, when a hip throw is employed, the opponent turns his back into you and pulls you to the right front corner by your right arm which is pulled tightly across his chest. Now, if the opponent can keep your body bent forward and close to his body, he can easily control you. As the opponent turns his back into you, his weight comes to rest on his left foot, making him weak to his left rear corner. To avoid the move, stand straight, abdomen forward, with your weight shifted to your left leg, and push him away with your arms. This prevents your form from being broken, places a counterforce to your left side, and creates a space between you and the opponent so that he cannot control your body. Now, if the opponent is strong and pulls you forward with a sudden jerk, you can create the same basic counterconditions as follows: quickly pull your right arm back, using shoulder power, and turn your body clockwise, bringing the right hip and leg back. At the same time shift your weight to your left leg and push against his left thigh with your left hand. You will not only stop his action but may also cause him to lean back to his left side. Then with your hands you can easily throw him down on his back in front of your left leg. Now, if the opponent pulls you off balance to your right front corner, you will be on your right leg, and the left leg will naturally come up behind you as you tip forward. At this point it is difficult and too late to shift your body to the left. If you can catch a solid support with your left leg he cannot throw you forward. The most solid support near you is his left leg which now bears both his and your weight. Therefore, stick your left leg stiffly out forward between his legs, bringing it against the inside of his left lower leg. This will stop his action completely, for if he throws you his left leg must also go, and this is not very likely.

A counter-throw may be employed not only to escape the throw but also to defeat the opponent. When the opponent turns his back into you, he is usually stiff as he attempts to throw you. Therefore, as you stop his action by one of the above methods, reach around his waist and bounce his body up and forward with the power of your abdomen and legs. Quickly throw him to the ground with *ushiro-goshi* or *utsuri-goshi*.

CHAPTER **5**

ashi-waza : leg throws

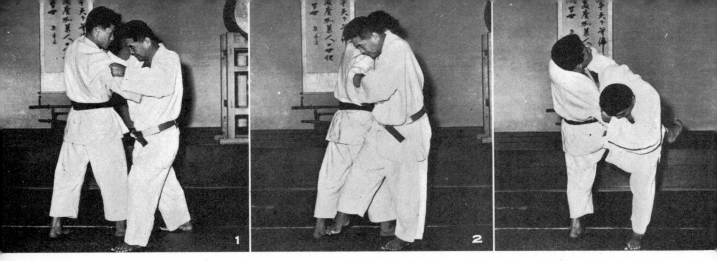

o-soto-gari: major outer-reaping throw

This technique requires that you bring the opponent's balance toward his rear so that his weight rests on one leg. Then the supporting leg is swept forward and the opponent is thrown on his back. The most difficult and important task is not the sweeping, but the timing and bringing the opponent into position.

Figures 1–3. Hold the opponent in the right natural position and lead him toward you. Normally as his right foot advances your left foot retreats. But when the opponent takes a definite step forward with his right foot, keep your weight on your right foot and slide your left foot forward to the outside of his right. At the same time pull the opponent up and against your body tightly. By pulling his right arm into your stomach with your left hand and lifting his body up and inward with your right hand, the opponent's weight will be made to come to his right foot. At this time roll your right hip forward, swinging your right leg behind the opponent's right leg. With your toes pointed downward, strike the back of the opponent's right calf low with your right calf and sweep upward. Keeping your body in line with your right leg, drive your right shoulder down against the opponent, trying to touch the mat with your forehead, as the leg sweeps upward. All movements should be executed quickly and simultaneously. If the opponent's weight is on both legs, then he is stronger than you as you are on one leg, and he can easily counter-throw you.

Figures 4–8. The only difference in this application is in the unbalancing of the opponent. Start by pushing against the opponent's left shoulder with your right hand, making him take a step backward. Then simultaneously slide your left foot to the outside of his right foot and pull with your right hand, making his left foot come forward. *Important:* as his left foot comes forward and before it touches the mat, push up with your right hand and pull in with your left hand. The hand motion will set his weight on his right foot and bring his body close to you. Closeness is important in order to control the opponent's body and to keep it unbalanced to your advantage. Throw as described above.

The opponent may attempt to stop you by shifting his weight to his left leg. At this moment firmly catch his neck with your right hand and push toward his back, making his weight come to the right foot again. Quickly sweep his leg, bending your body forward with force. Sometimes, if you cannot sweep his leg, hop forward, pushing him backward, and hook his right leg from behind with your right leg.

It may happen that in avoiding this technique the opponent will move his right leg backward. At this time you may apply *harai-goshi* or *uchimata.*

Figures 9–10. Here you grip the opponent's right collar with your right hand. Step forward deeply with your left foot and push the opponent back with both arms. As the opponent's balance is broken to his right rear corner, sweep his right leg.

Figures 11-13. When the opponent steps to his right, either sideways or at an angle, it is easy to unbalance him in that direction. This is done by sliding your left foot, knee slightly bent, in the same direction as his right foot is moving in, pointing your toes in that direction. Quickly pull his body up and against your body, making him tip to his right. With his weight completely on the right leg, sweep his leg, striking as low as possible.

COUNTER-TECHNIQUES

Figure 14. The simplest way to avoid this move is to lift your right leg forward, shifting your weight to your left leg. As you can lift your leg higher forward than the opponent can lift his leg backward, it is easy to avoid his sweep.

Another way of stopping the opponent is to push forward, keeping the opponent from coming in close. If the opponent is in close and has already started to sweep, quickly shift your weight forward on your left leg, bending your head forward in that direction. Try to step forward with your left foot if possible. The weight of your head in addition to the pressure of your body will shift your center of gravity to your left front, countering the opponent's force.

Figures 15-16. To counter-throw an opponent, step back with your left leg just as he starts to sweep his right leg. Shifting your weight to the left leg, pull his body strongly against your body and quickly sweep his leg with your right leg. This technique is *o-soto-gari* but it is used as a counter-throw in this case.

o-soto-otoshi: major outer drop

This technique is similar to *o-soto-gari* in that you step behind the opponent and throw him backward. However, when the opponent assumes a defensive position and his balance is on both legs it will not be possible to throw by sweeping as in *o-soto-gari*. Therefore, pull the opponent forward, taking a step to his right side with your left foot. As he counters your pull by trying to rise, lift your right leg, knee well bent. Slide your foot alongside his right buttock and down behind him to a point between his legs, pointing your toes back toward you. At the same time pull his body tightly against your body, and then drive him back into the mat using the force of your right shoulder against his right shoulder. The drive of your leg behind his buttock will make his knees buckle and throw his center of gravity to his rear. Counter-techniques for this move are the same as for *o-soto-gari*.

o-soto-guruma: major outer-wheel throw

This is similar to *o-soto-gari*, except that you sweep both of the opponent's legs at the same time. In order to apply this technique both of the opponent's legs should be fairly close together, his heels carrying his weight. The first move is to pull the opponent forward with your right hand and to step to the outside of his right foot with your left foot. This basic position can be obtained by directly stepping in; or by advancing slightly with your left foot as the opponent steps forward with his right; or by taking a long sliding step forward with your left foot as the opponent steps back with his right foot; or by recovering your balance with your left foot by his right foot after attempting an unsuccessful foot sweep with your left foot against his right foot. Next, as your left foot comes into position, pull his right elbow into your body and pull and lift his left shoulder with your right hand. As he resists he will lean back on his heels. At this time roll your right hip forward, bringing your leg across the back of both of his legs. Quickly sweep the opponent's legs forward, driving his back to the mat with your hands and the power of your right shoulder against his.

Counter-techniques for this move are the same as for *o-soto-gari*.

ko-soto-gari : minor outer-reaping throw

The success of this move depends upon bringing the weight of the opponent on one heel and sweeping that leg out from under him while at the same time he is pushed back and down with your hands. Move to his right side by sliding one step forward with your left foot. At the same time pull him down by his right arm and lift his left shoulder up by giving a circular pull-and-lift motion with your arms. This pull will twist his upper body, and he will now stand on his right foot, with his balance centered on his right heel. Now, quickly shift your weight from your left to right leg, bending the right knee slightly, and sweep the opponent's right foot with your left foot. Strike the back of his heel with the sole of your foot, sweeping it forward in the direction of his toes. Simultaneously, straighten your right leg and push him on his back with your hands. To attain the basic position in this move, you may push the opponent's right arm, making him step back on his right foot. At that time take a step forward with your left foot, shifting his balance to his right rear corner, and then apply the move.

If the opponent stands in the natural position it will be difficult to apply this move. Therefore, pull him forward a few times. As he steps forward his legs will spread a little, and he will be forced to lean forward. To resist your pull, he will draw backward. Taking advantage of his counter-force, take a short step forward with your right foot and push him back with your hands. This double force will make him stand on his heels, weakening his position. Quickly, keeping your balance on your right foot, sweep his right heel with your left foot as described above and drive his back to the mat.

When *tsurikomi-goshi* fails this move may be applied. When this move fails, you can suddenly drop to the mat and apply *yoko-sutemi*.

COUNTER-TECHNIQUES

To stop the opponent, push him away with your arms. If he breaks your balance, then pull with your right arm and push with your left arm, leaning to your left front corner. A counter-throw is difficult to apply, but you can use *yoko-sutemi*, falling to your left side.

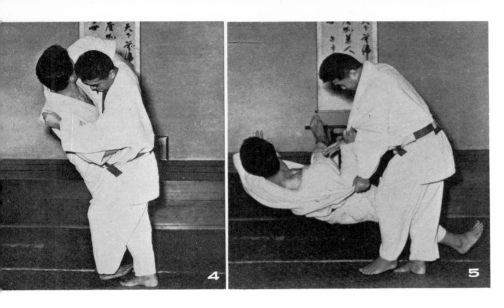

o-uchi-gari: *major inner-reaping throw*

Figures 1-3. If the opponent stands in the natural position it will be difficult to apply this move successfully as he can easily regain his balance. Therefore, it should be your aim to make him stand in a position in which he cannot shift his balance easily from one leg to the other. This can be done by pulling him so that he steps forward with his left foot, standing in a defensive position with legs wide apart. Still pulling the opponent, take half a step back and around with your left leg, bending the knee for balance. Twisting your right hip close to his body, introduce your right leg between his legs and sweep his left leg forward in a circular motion. In sweeping, be careful that you strike his calf muscle with your calf and not behind the knee joint with the back of your knee. For, in the latter case, the position of his leg below the knee is free and he will be able to apply a counter-throw on you instead. As his leg is swept off the mat, apply a violent push to his left rear corner, throwing him on his back. The push may be more effective if you change your grip and push him down with your palms pressing against his body.

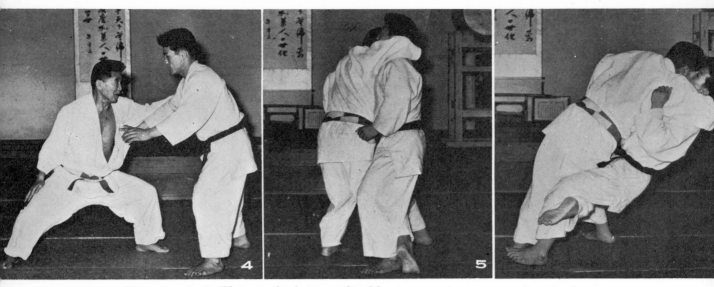

Figures 4-6. This method is applicable in actual contests when both parties stand in a defensive position in order to avoid being thrown by the other. For success in this move it is necessary to disturb the calmness of your opponent. For this proceed as follows: first stand in the defensive posture, the opponent will also assume this posture. Now, firmly catch the right sleeve of your opponent with your left hand. Suddenly, slap your right hand against your right thigh and shout. The sound will momentarily shock and puzzle the opponent. Taking advantage of this moment pull him forward by his right arm, and suddenly leap toward him and hook your right arm around his neck, pulling his head into your chest. Then sweep his left leg with your right as previously described. Generally, when you catch him like this, he will try to escape, not knowing what to do, by pulling himself up. This is also a good opportunity. Fall violently on him as both bodies spring up and drive his back to the mat.

Another opportunity occurs when the opponent attempts to use a leg move on you. At this time grip one of his legs, lifting it off the mat, then sweep his supporting leg with *o-uchi-gari*.

Figures 7-8. *O-uchi-gari* is used many times in combination with other techniques. In the example shown, if you have tried *o-uchi-gari* and have failed because the opponent raised his leg to escape, you quickly apply *tai-otoshi* on his supporting leg.

COUNTER-TECHNIQUES

Figures 9-10. Standing in the natural position will prevent the successful application of *o-uchi-gari*. Normally, when the opponent hooks his right leg and sweeps your left, you can easily escape by shifting your weight to your right leg. Quickly turn your left leg with the heel up. If he leans to his right side, you can throw him on his back by pulling with your left hand and pushing with your right hand in a circular motion toward your left side. As his right leg is off the ground and hooked by your left leg he can easily be thrown to his right by your hand motion and by sweeping his leg across to your right.

Figures 11-12. When the opponent shoves you to the left back side as he sweeps your leg, fall quickly to your left side and throw him over your left shoulder with *yoko-sutemi*.

If you are successful in avoiding his sweep, then, as his leg swings back and up, his weight will be on his left leg. You can immediately cross your left foot in front of his left leg and apply *tai-otoshi* as shown in Figures 7–8.

ashi-waza : 63

ashi-guruma: leg wheel throw

This technique although similar to *harai-goshi* differs from it in that the hip is not used for power. Suppose the opponent stands with his right leg back. Take a quick step to the front of his left foot with your left foot and pull his body up to the front so that he stands on his toes. Now, pivoting on your left foot, bring your right leg diagonally across the front of his body and place it against his right knee joint. This stops the motion of his right leg, and his knee is used as a fulcrum to pivot his body across your leg. Give a small circular pull to his right hand in the direction of your left toe, also lifting and pulling with your right arm. Because you have placed your right leg on his right knee, he will not be able to move that leg. Your pull will twist his body, and he will fall over your leg in front of you. Remember to keep your right leg stiff and sweep back with it as you throw the opponent.

The same move can be applied when the opponent moves with his right leg forward. Stop his motion with your left hand and step across to his left with your left foot. Then, pivoting on the left foot, apply the move as described above.

This move may be applied when *harai-goshi* (Figures 3–4) fails or *harai-goshi* may be applied when *ashi-guruma* fails.

Counter-techniques for this move are similar to those employed against most hip throws.

ko-uchi-gari: minor inner-reaping throw

This technique is similar to *o-uchi-gari* except that you sweep the opponent's right foot with your right foot instead of his left foot as in *o-uchi-gari*. Again, it is important that the opponent's weight be on the heel of the foot you attack.

Figures 1-6. This is the basic method of applying *ko-uchi-gari*. Pull the opponent's right arm so that he takes a large step forward with his right foot and spreads his legs wide apart. In this position it is difficult for him to shift his weight to his left foot. At this moment, take a step back with your left foot behind your right foot, still pulling the opponent forward. Quickly shift your weight to your left leg and, bending the knee for balance, sweep the heel of the opponent's right foot with the sole of your right foot. Strike his heel low in the direction of his toes. Simultaneously pull down and push back with your hands, driving his back to the mat. It is important that the sole of your foot maintains control of the opponent's right foot at all times so that his leg cannot escape. Also, you must throw him on his back as it is not considered a completed throw if he touches the mat with his buttocks first.

Figures 7-10. Generally, a good judo-man will keep his weight on his back leg and not on his front leg because this is dangerous. If you apply *ko-uchi-gari* while the opponent's weight is on his back leg he will be able to counter-throw you or escape. The following illustrations show how to attack the opponent's rear leg when he assumes a right defensive position. In this case you must also assume the right defensive position for your own protection. Now in this position it is difficult to sweep his left foot because of the great distance between your left foot and his. Therefore, step forward with your right foot to a point midway between his legs, pulling him toward you. Quickly sweep his left heel with your left foot and drive him to the mat with your chest against his chest. A stronger method of using the hands is to grip the opponent's jacket near the armpits. Then, as you apply the move, spread your elbows, making him raise his arms and lean backward.

Figures 11-12. Another method is used when the opponent leads you sideways, say, to your left. Move sideways with the opponent, then, just as his right foot touches the mat, change the grip of your right hand to his left collar above the shoulder. Press down hard with both hands and quickly sweep his right foot with your right foot.

Figures 13-15. If the opponent keeps his body in a natural position, it is often difficult to apply this move directly. Therefore, *ko-uchi-gari* is commonly used in combination with another move. First apply *o-uchi-gari* to the opponent's left leg, then as he lifts the leg to escape, quickly apply *ko-uchi-gari* to his right supporting leg.

Figures 16 & 17. These illustrations show a few ways of controlling the opponent's body when applying the technique. Methods such as these have their use during contests, when force is necessary.

COUNTER-TECHNIQUES

To avoid *ko-uchi-gari* it is absolutely necessary that you stand in the natural position. If your legs are spread apart the opponent will probably be successful. When the opponent sweeps your right leg with his right, lift your leg up and forward, removing it from his foot. Remember you can move your leg higher forward than he can lift his own leg backward. You can prevent his leg from catching yours by twisting his body to your right as he attempts to apply the move.

Figures 18-20. To counter-throw the opponent as he sweeps up your left foot, press the sole of your left foot against his ankle and apply *sasae-tsurikomi-ashi-harai.* Pull up and around with your hands as you sweep his foot, thereby lifting him off the mat and throwing him. A similar counter-throw can be performed by placing your foot on his knee and applying *hiza-guruma.*

uchi-mata: inner thigh sweep

The success of this move depends on placing your thigh as far in as possible between the opponent's thighs and lifting him off the ground, throwing him down with the power of your hands, hip, and thigh. If the opponent stands in the natural position, he will be difficult to throw; his legs, therefore, should be made to spread apart, or his weight should be made to rest on one leg.

Figures 1-3. Pull the opponent sideways with your right arm, making him take a step toward your right side. As soon as his right leg touches the mat, step back and around with your left foot, between and to the front of the opponent's legs, keeping your knee well bent. Quickly pull his body close to you and swing your right thigh up deep between his thighs. The back of your right thigh should strike the inside of his left thigh, raising his legs off the mat. Pull with your left hand and turn your body to the left, keeping your head low and well in front to your right side.

Figures 4-6. Another method is to jump into position. When the opponent is in the defensive position, break his balance to the front by pulling him forward sharply with force. Then, keeping your left knee well bent, jump in low and deep between his legs and throw him. When jumping in, your left foot comes against the opponent's right foot, your toes pointing in the same direction as his. As the left foot comes into place, your right leg springs up between the opponent's thighs. Straighten your left knee as you raise the opponent.

Figures 7-9. In some cases the opponent's defensive position is so low that you cannot enter in the normal way. Give your opponent a sudden jerk forward as if you were going to attack. Then, in order to make his position stronger, he will stiffen and spread his legs more. At this moment jump into position with the back of your right knee striking and lifting behind his left knee. As he is raised, pull up with your right arm and down across your chest with your left arm in a circular motion. Roll your body hard to the left and, if this does not throw him, let your body roll to the mat, taking him with you.

Another method is needed when you apply *seoi-nage* and are unsuccessful: spring your thigh between his legs, throwing him with what is called *seoi-uchi-mata*.

COUNTER-TECHNIQUES

Because of the large movements the opponent has to make, and the fact that he has to rest his weight on one leg, there are many possibilities for defense or counter-throwing. As you can raise your left leg higher forward than he can raise his right leg backward, you can sometimes escape in this way.

Figure 10. By keeping your legs together, you make it difficult for him to apply this move. Just as his leg enters between yours, clamp your knees together, catching his leg and stopping his action.

He may succeed in entering deep with his leg and raising you off the mat. In this case, catch his left inner thigh from the outside with your left hand, and, spreading your legs, lean your upper body forward. Press him strongly with your weight on his right side and pull your body close to him with your left hand. This action will make it difficult for him to lift you, and since you have your legs spread you will not fall even if he twists his body and tries to take you to the mat with him.

14

15

Figures 11-13. Another method of escaping is to turn your body quickly by stepping back with your left foot as he sweeps, causing him to miss your body completely. His right leg therefore sweeps high in the air, and he is brought forward on his left foot. Quickly pull with your right hand and push with the left, turning his body like a wheel. Sometimes this hand motion alone will throw him. However, you can easily bend low with your left foot across his left leg and apply *tai-otoshi* (Figure 14).

Figure 15. Avoiding his sweep as described above, apply *harai-tsurikomi-ashi* by quickly sweeping the front of his left ankle with your right foot.

11   12   13

kani-waza: scissors technique

This technique is applied just as a crab fights by keeping its balance on one side of its body and catching its enemy with its legs in a scissors grip. Pull the opponent's right hand so that he takes a step forward with his right foot, making his body turn in a half-right direction. You are now in line with his right side. Step back and around with your right foot and touch the mat with your right hand by your right foot. Always keep pulling with your left hand to make the opponent lean to his right side. Now, quickly scissor his body deeply, placing your right leg behind both of his calf-muscles and your left leg across his pelvis. Throw the opponent backward by pushing to his front with your right leg, back with your left leg, and pulling back with your left hand.

A good chance to apply *kani-waza* is when the opponent attempts to get a hold on you and moves his right leg forward to do so. This puts you in line with his right side, and at this moment quickly touch the mat behind you with your right hand and apply the move as described above.

COUNTER-TECHNIQUES

In order to escape this move, spread your legs with one leg forward. This will prevent him from throwing you with a scissors grip. By dropping down you can hold the opponent with a grappling technique *(ne-waza)*.

  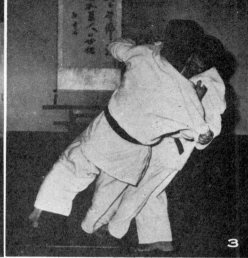

de-ashi-barai: advanced foot sweep

As the name implies, you sweep the opponent's foot as it advances. When sweeping try to curve your foot inward like the palm of your hand, so that the whole strength of your body below the waist comes to your little toe. Now pull your opponent so that his right foot comes forward. If his foot touches the mat, it will be difficult to sweep. Therefore, just as his right foot starts to touch the mat, you sweep it forward by striking the right rear of his foot under the ankle with the ball of your foot. At the same time lift up with both hands in a circular motion, raising him off the mat as you sweep, then throw him on his back.

Another application of this move may be made when you have swept one leg, and the opponent lifts up that leg to escape. Continue your hold and sweep the back of his supporting leg before the first leg returns to the mat.

okuri-ashi-harai: sliding foot sweep

As the opponent walks sideways, say to his left, his right leg will follow his left leg with every other step. At this point he is weakest. Follow the opponent's steps by stepping sideways with him. As his right foot moves toward his left, push in on his right elbow and lift his right shoulder in a circular motion, tipping his body up and to his right. Simultaneously, sweep his right foot with your left foot, striking just under his ankle with the ball of your foot.

Sometimes you face the difficulty of the opponent not moving farther to his left and taking a firm stand. At this time you will take a longer step sideways with your right foot, making him follow you. Then as he follows, you apply the move as described above.

sasae-tsurikomi-ashi-harai:
propping-lifting foot sweep

The nature of this technique is to support or prop your foot against the opponent's ankle, using it as a pivot point and throwing him by using your hands and feet together. As the opponent pushes you backward and takes a step forward with his left foot, move backward making half a turn clockwise and stepping outside his right foot with your left foot, pointing your toes inward. Your weight now rests on your left foot. Place the sole of your right foot against the front of his right ankle, stopping its forward motion. Throw by lifting up with your left hand and down with your right in a circular motion just as his body is tipped forward. To apply this move the opponent does not necessarily have to push you, for you can pull him forward, then, stepping back and turning your left foot in diagonally, you can apply the move. The position of your right hand can also be changed to his left elbow for better leverage.

harai-tsurikomi-ashi: lifting foot sweep

This technique is quite similar to *sasae-tsurikomi-ashi-harai,* except that you step in between the opponent's legs and lift him somewhat higher. Push the opponent by his left shoulder; then naturally his left leg will move back. At this moment slide your left leg between his legs directly under him, bringing your entire weight to your left leg. Quickly lift the opponent up and forward so that his balance comes up on his toes. Now, twist his body with the motion of your hands to your right side and sweep the sole of your right foot against his left front ankle, thereby throwing him. This move can also be applied when the opponent pushes your left shoulder, stepping forward with his right foot. At this moment step between his legs with your left foot and apply the move.

sasae-okuri-ashi-harai: propping-sliding foot sweep

This technique is used as a follow-up move to an unsuccessful *sasae-tsurikomi ashi*, when the opponent pulls his left foot back to avoid the move. At the moment he does so, pull him up and forward so that his weight comes across your right thigh and hip. Now you sweep his left leg, or you may sweep both legs toward his right side. It is important that your left foot be turned slightly inward throughout the throw, as it supports your weight when you pivot on it. Do not bend your body but keep it straight when sweeping.

hiza-guruma: knee wheel throw

This move is similar to *sasae-tsurikomi-ashi* except that you apply pressure to the opponent's knee rather than to his ankle. As the opponent steps forward with his right foot, step slightly back and to the outside of his right foot with your left foot, toes pointed inward. Then, just as he starts to bring his left foot forward, place your right foot on his left kneecap. Keeping pressure on his knee, throw by pulling his left shoulder forward and lifting his right arm in a circular motion. This will twist his body over your right foot. You may also apply your right foot to his left knee as he plants his left foot forward on the mat.

COUNTER-TECHNIQUES

If the opponent applies *hiza-guruma* on your left knee, then spread your left leg, dropping your body low. Pull him forward by his left arm with your right, and he will be forced to take his right foot off your knee. To counter-throw, catch his raised foot with your left hand and hook your right foot from the inside behind his supporting leg, sweeping it forward. This is an application of *o-uchi-gari*.

counter-techniques for ashi-waza

The basic method for avoiding foot sweeping moves is to bring back the leg which is being swept and avoid the opponent's foot, pushing him away from you simultaneously. In order to bring your foot back, it is only necessary to bend your leg at the knee as this is fast and does not telegraph your movement to the opponent. Simultaneously, shift your weight to the other foot. When the opponent applies a foot sweep his weight is entirely on one foot making his position weak. In order to counter-throw the opponent, it is best if you sweep his supporting foot out from under him or counter-sweep his sweeping foot.

Figures 1–3. This counter-sweep is called *tsubame-gaeshi* (swallow-counter). The name "swallow" is given because the motion of your lower leg is like the flight of a swallow. When the opponent applies *de-ashi-harai* to your left foot, quickly bring your foot back, avoiding the sweep, and in a circular motion swing it back, sweeping his foot which has just missed. At the same time, lift and pull the opponent to his right as you sweep his foot, as in the application of *de-ashi-harai*. This is a difficult counter-throw, and can only be used if you are good at applying *de-ashi-harai*. Constant practice is necessary for the successful execution of this move.

Figures 4–5. This counter-sweep is applied after the opponent has missed your foot when attempting *de-ashi-harai*. In this case you sweep his supporting foot from behind. This move is also an application of *de-ashi-harai*.

Figures 6–7. When the opponent attempts a move like *sasae-ashi* or *harai-tsurikomi-ashi* on your left foot, pull the foot back. Quickly sweep his supporting foot from behind with your left foot, pushing him with your hands toward his right rear corner where he is weak.

CHAPTER **6**

sutemi-waza:
back and side throws

tomoe-nage: summersault throw

Figures 1–7. This is one of the most basic and strongest methods of throwing a person when throwing yourself backward *(sutemi-waza)*. There should be a space between the contestants and they may or may not have one foot in front of the other. In this case the opponent's right foot is forward. If the opponent is not stepping or bending forward to begin with, then start by pushing him back. He will resist, setting up a counter-force toward his front. At this moment apply the move as follows: change your hold by gripping both of his arms by the elbows, and press both of his arms together. This gives you control of his arms, and prevents him from using them to escape the throw. Simultaneously, slide your left leg deep between his legs, lying down on your back and bending your right leg back against your chest. Be careful not to allow your buttocks to touch the ground first as this will keep you from pulling him forward and he may escape. Therefore, lie down, touching the mat with your back first, and place the ball of your right foot below his abdomen. Now, applying strength to your left foot, straighten your right leg and throw him over your head. As you throw, keep his elbows pulled in so that he cannot stand on his hands and escape. Also, it is important that you pull with your hands in a circular motion, pulling your arms back toward you as he is thrown overhead. This will prevent him from landing on his head or escaping and assures you a good clean throw.

Figures 8-9. When the opponent is too heavy, and you cannot throw him over your head, then the following can be done. Help your right foot by placing the ball of your left foot near the right side of his abdomen and raise him with both feet. Then, twisting your body to the right, push up strongly with your left foot and hand, pulling in with your right hand. This will roll his body as he is thrown up and he will fall on your right side.

COUNTER-TECHNIQUES

Figure 10. As the opponent drops down on his back, and before his foot touches your abdomen, quickly drop down on your knee, thus preventing his upward thrust. You can also avoid his foot by turning your upper body sideways.

Figures 11-12. When the opponent throws you, his push continues only up to the point where you are standing head down perpendicular to his body. At this point, touch the ground or his chest with your hands, and, twisting your body in mid-air, land on your feet just over his head or to the side.

sumi-gaeshi: corner throw

When the opponent is in the defensive position grasping you about the waist, assume the same position. You may either grasp the opponent by his belt or under his armpits as shown in the illustrations. The opponent will either push you backward or pull you forward. As the opponent steps forward with his right foot, you step back and outside his right with your left foot. Simultaneously, drop to the mat on your back pulling him with you. This will make his balance come forward on his toes. Throw him over your left shoulder by placing your right lower leg against his left inner thigh, pushing up with your leg, and pulling with your arms. Also, employ your hip power by arching your back and pushing with your left foot.

This technique is also useful when the opponent is standing over you attempting to apply a choking or holding technique.

tawara-gaeshi: bale throw

This throw is much like lifting a bale of straw by putting both arms around it and using your lower abdomen for lifting. When the opponent reaches low around your legs or waist, move back so that his head drops down by your lower abdomen. Then reach around his waist, pulling him in toward you. Spread your legs and drop down on your back, buttocks first. In doing so snap your abdomen forward and lift with your arms, throwing him over either of your shoulders. Do not throw him directly behind you as there is danger of his landing on your face.

This move can also be applied when you unsuccessfully try to throw the opponent forward from a standing position, or when he tries to attack you when you are lying on the ground.

ura-nage: back throw

This, like *tomoe-nage*, requires that you throw yourself on your back when throwing the opponent. This technique is an effective means of defense when an opponent attacks you with an overhead swing of his right arm. As the contestants, however, do not strike each other in judo, this technique is usually and most effectively used when the opponent, while trying to apply a throwing technique, turns his right side into your front. Place the palm of your left hand firmly against his back belt and your right palm against his left front belt. Pressing your palms firmly, pull his right side into your chest and bend your knees deeply. Quickly, with an upward lift of your abdomen and hands, throw him over your left shoulder, falling on your back as you do so. If the opponent resists and tries to bend forward to escape, then take a few short steps backward on your heels. This will carry him in your direction, and just as his weight shifts toward you apply the move.

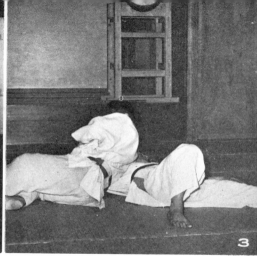

soto-makikomi: outer winding throw

This throw is similar to most hip throws except that you hold one of the opponent's arms with both of your arms and roll your body, falling to the mat with the opponent as you throw him.

Pull the opponent's right arm tightly across your chest with your left hand. Then release the grip of your right hand and bring it over the top of his right arm, clamping it against your right side. At the same time step to the outside of his right foot with your right foot, stopping its forward motion. Throw the opponent over your right hip by winding your body counterclockwise and falling to the mat with him. If the opponent takes a step forward with his right foot to escape, you step back and around with your left foot and continue to roll him to the mat. Then if the opponent pulls back with his right shoulder, hook your right arm against the left side of his head and neck, forcing his head forward, and then apply the move.

uchi-makikomi: inner winding throw

Uchi-makikomi is similar to *soto-makikomi* except that you hook your right arm under the opponent's right arm for control. It is not necessary to step across his right foot; just bend your knees and straighten them as you roll and throw the opponent. This move is useful when *ippon-seoi-nage* is first attempted and fails.

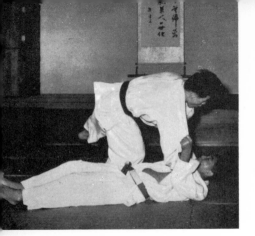

yoko-ware: side separation throw

This move is applied as the opponent makes a quick movement forward. At this moment, quickly drop to the mat as shown in the illustration, throwing the opponent over you with a strong circular motion of your hands.

uki-waza: floating technique

This is the basic method of throwing the opponent by falling on your side. Move the opponent forward so that he takes definite steps forward, lifting him upward as you do so. As the opponent steps forward with his right foot, shifting his weight to it, quickly drop to your left side, sliding your left leg deeply forward across the front of his right foot. This will stop the motion of his right foot, and the force of your fall will make him tip forward. Pull hard in a circular motion, pulling the opponent's right shoulder into you as you throw him. This will prevent him from falling on his shoulder and injuring it, and also it will help to control his body when he is thrown. Spring against the mat with your right foot and arch your back for power as you throw.

This move can also be applied when the opponent pushes you back or when he moves sideways. In the latter event, pull down with one arm and up with the other, tipping him sideways like a wheel, then drop to the mat and throw as described above.

tani-otoshi: valley drop

This technique can be applied when you and the opponent grip each other deeply in low defensive positions. First, step slightly forward with your right foot, pushing the opponent toward his left rear corner. As he resists, quickly drop to the mat, sliding your left foot forward. Throw the opponent to your right side, using the power of your arms and body.

yoko-gakae: side breaking throw

This move is applied by sweeping the opponent's leg and falling to the mat with him. Pull the opponent's right arm forward continuously until he is balanced forward on his right foot. When he is in this position, sweep away his right foot with the sole of your left foot, striking the outside of his right foot. Fall simultaneously to the ground on your left side, continuing to pull his right hand as you fall. The force of your fall, the power of your pull, and the sweeping of your foot will throw him to the mat. After falling, maintain your hold and watch the opponent as you may have to continue fighting on the mat if it was not a successful throw.

PART III

ne-waza:
grappling techniques

CHAPTER 7

preparation for ne-waza

We have already discussed *tachi-waza*, or fighting from a standing position. This is the way fighting usually starts, but often it ends up on the ground. A person is in a more natural element when he is standing, and it is easier for him to defend himself in this position. A good judo-man must be able to fight as well on the ground as when standing. The advantage of ground fighting is that the movements are slower and more cautious, which allows you time to rest and build up energy for the decisive moves. Also, the average person is relatively helpless when fighting from a lying position, and if you have developed this ability it will be relatively easy to defeat your opponent. In judo, *ne-waza* is used when one or both of the opponents fall to the mat after an unsuccessful attempt to throw each other. Generally, rules prohibit taking your opponent directly to the mat for the sake of engaging him in *ne-waza*. However, judo-men who are good at *ne-waza* usually will apply a throw with the intent of bringing the opponent down to the mat. *Ne-waza* consists of three general methods of fighting:

1. *Osaekomi-waza:* holding techniques. The purpose of these techniques is to hold or immobilize your opponent on his back for a period of thirty seconds.
2. *Shime-waza:* strangling holds. Here the object is to strangle the opponent by pressure against the side of his neck until he surrenders or blacks out.
3. *Kansetsu-waza:* armlock techniques. The object is to apply pressure to the opponent's elbow joint, making him surrender because of the severe pain. In judo pressure on the elbow joint alone is allowed, as pressure on any other joint is considered too dangerous for a sport.

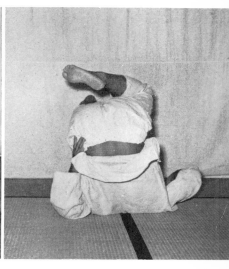

calisthenics for ne-waza

Before you can practice holding methods, you first must learn how to assume a natural position on the mat. As in standing techniques, a natural position is one which gives you the greatest degree of flexibility and strength. There are many positions that can be used to advantage when lying on the mat. In each case, however, your body must be supple and able to move about freely, allowing you to shift your weight and position as the situation may demand. In order to accustom your body to the mat and to the movements peculiar to ground fighting, it is necessary that you exercise for this purpose. The illustrations on this page will give an idea of some of the special movements required to supplement ordinary calisthenics. You should practice bridging your back and turning from side to side. It is also necessary that you develop strong neck muscles for bridging, and for pulling your body along the mat, using also your shoulders, arms, and legs.

postures on the mat

As in *tachi-waza,* or techniques from a standing position, there are certain basic postures for *ne-waza.* When you hold an opponent, he will struggle and try to escape. In doing so he will twist and turn his body, changing his position in relation to you. Generally it is very difficult to hold a strong opponent in one fixed position. You must be able to move about with the opponent, controlling his movements while retaining a strong position yourself. When holding, keep your body relaxed and apply pressure only to his center of gravity. It is well known that if a piece of wood floating on

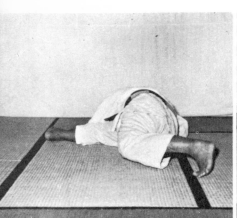  

water is pressed down at any point other than its center of gravity it will flip over. Your relationship to the opponent on the mat is similar to that of you and the piece of floating wood. It is important to keep in mind that, no matter how powerful he may be, a person cannot raise his body at once if you are lying across him. He must therefore apply power from one point of his body at a time, thus trying to unbalance you in relation to himself. Therefore, **bide yo**ur time in a relaxed position and apply pressure against his center of gravity or whichever part of his body he tries to raise. The position of your body should always be such that he will find it difficult to upset you. Use your arms and legs as supports so that you cannot be tipped in any direction.

94 : ne-waza

attacking and controlling the opponent

Before you can apply any hold on the opponent you must be able to break his defense and control his body. This presents one of the greatest problems in *osaekomi-waza*, for once you have obtained control over the opponent's body more than half the fight is won. Remember to maintain control of at least one part of the opponent's body at all times so that he cannot escape.

Figures 1-4. You have thrown the opponent and still control his right arm. Grasp his right collar with your right hand thus controlling his right shoulder. In order to keep him from turning or bringing his right knee between you and himself for escaping, place your right foot and knee into his right side. Now you may apply *kami-shiho-gatame* or some other form of hold.

Figures 5-8. Here you have thrown the opponent, but you do not have control of his right arm. Reach across his left shoulder with your left arm and seize his jacket or belt along his left side, using your shoulder to flatten his body. Now he will try to bring his right knee up between you and him. To prevent this slide your right hand, palm down, under his right thigh, controlling its movement. Spread your legs and, rising on your toes, counter the upward push of his left shoulder and you complete the hold *(kuzure kami-shiho-gatame)*.

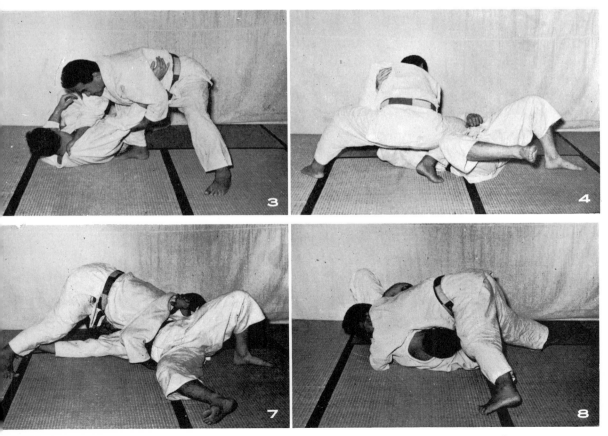

Figures 9-14. In this case the opponent is in a defensive position, on guard with his legs raised. Enter deep between his legs, reaching under his left thigh and grasping his belt with your right hand. Your left hand covers the top of his right thigh, grasping his trouser leg, preventing him from raising his leg. Raise his left leg with your right hand and push down his right leg as you step around to his right side. Now reach over his left thigh with your right arm and grasp his belt, using your elbow at the same time to keep in his left leg. Note how the left knee is used in Figure 14 to control the opponent's body, and how the right leg is brought back for stability. Next reach with your left hand deep behind his collar or over his left shoulder (Figure 14) to control his upper body, while maintaining control of his lower body with your knee and right hand. Then slide your right hand, palm down, under his right thigh, and you are in position for a good hold (*kuzure-yoko-shiho-gatame*).

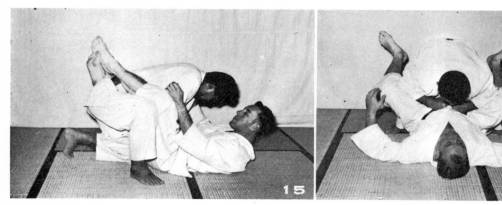

Figures 15-20. The opponent encircles your waist with his legs. You grasp the front of his belt with both hands, then raise him a little. Next, drop down with force, spreading your elbows against the inside of his thighs. Also spread your knees for additional power. This will make the opponent spread his legs, releasing his hold. Reach under his left thigh with your right hand, grip his belt and lift his thigh and turn him on his right side with the power of your right arm and shoulder. At the same time step around to his left side with your right foot, then sit on the mat bringing your left foot from behind you. This brings you in a good position to apply a side hold such as *ushiro-kesa-gatame* or *yoko-shiho-gatame*.

Figures 21-24. The opponent cleverly wards you off with his feet. Grasp quickly the inside of his left trouser leg and do a cartwheel spring over his body across his right shoulder. Slide your left hand over his left shoulder, grasping his belt, and grasp his right outer trouser leg with your right hand. Now, spread your legs for balance and you have control of his body (*kuzure-yoko-shiho-gatame*).

Figures 25-27. Grasping both of the opponent's ankles, pull his legs back between yours and jump forward. You now can lie down on him, hooking your legs about the outside of his legs, and apply *tate-shiho-gatame*.

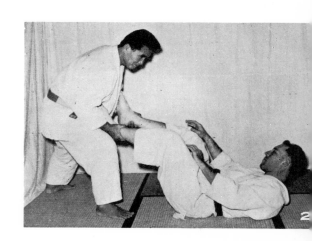

Figures 28-30. Catching the opponent's ankles, swing his legs from left to right, confusing him. Then quickly throw his legs away to one side, leaving his side open to your attack.

Figures 31-32. Grasp the opponent's ankles, pull his legs straight, and turn your body around backward which brings you alongside him.

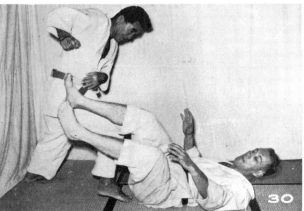

Figures 33-34. As the opponent tries to wrap his legs around you, slide your left arm under his right thigh, grasping his belt. With your right hand, bring your left hand over and around his left thigh and across to his right collar, grasping it deeply. Rise and set the opponent up on the back of his neck, which will cause him severe pain. You can either hold him there or turn your body around to his side for a better hold.

Figures 35-36. The opponent is lying on his stomach in a defensive position. Reach over him, grasping his clothes at the elbow and knee. Lift him up and turn his body over. You can grasp his clothes on the side toward you, but in this case he may catch your legs to avoid being turned over.

Figures 37-41. Here again the opponent lies on his stomach in a defensive position, gripping both sides of his collar to prevent being strangled. You are on his left side; slide your right hand under his body and grasp his right elbow. With your left hand grasp his right shoulder. Then with the power of your arms and feet turn him over on his back and quickly apply a hold *(kesa-gatame)*.

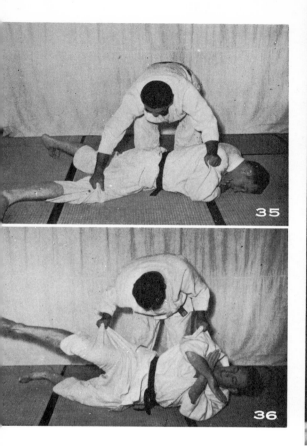

CHAPTER *8*

osaekomi-waza: holding techniques

*O*nce *you* have control of the opponent's body you can apply any of the following techniques. There are many modifications of each basic technique; these are denoted with the prefix *kuzure,* meaning "modified form." With each technique, counter-methods and escapes are shown, giving you a more complete understanding of the principles of *ne-waza.*

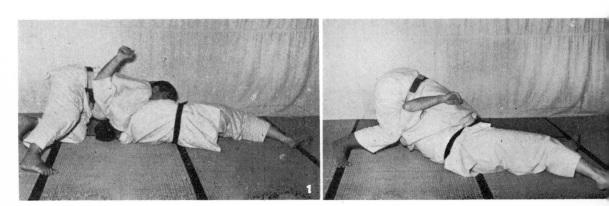

104 : ne-waza

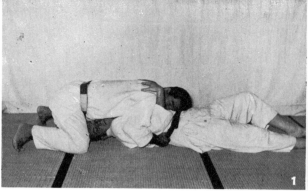

kami-shiho-gatame: upper four-corner hold

Approach the opponent from behind in a kneeling position. Spread your knees as wide as possible with your toes pointed outward so that the inner edges of your feet touch the mat. This will give you great stability, preventing the opponent from turning you over. Slide both of your hands under the opponent's arms along his sides and grip his belt tightly. Pull back with your arms, pressing the elbows inward tightly against his sides. At the same time press your stomach and chest firmly against his head and chest. This will immobilize the upper part of his body. Keep his head between your knees and press your stomach against his head. When the opponent tries to rise to remove his head from under you, then stand up on your toes, with feet spread wide apart. Sometimes you may achieve better results with one knee bent forward and the other leg stretched outward. Also, as he tries to turn his body, move along with him so as to maintain your body in a straight line with his.

kuzure-kami-shiho-gatame:
modified upper four-corner hold

Figures 1–4. This move is quite similar to the regular *kami-shiho-gatame* except that you bring your right arm over the top of his right arm and behind his neck, gripping the collar as far to the left as possible. Your body in this case lies on a line approximately 45 degrees to one side of his body. When the opponent tries to roll you toward your left shoulder, place your forehead against the mat along his left side as a support and come up on your toes simultaneously.

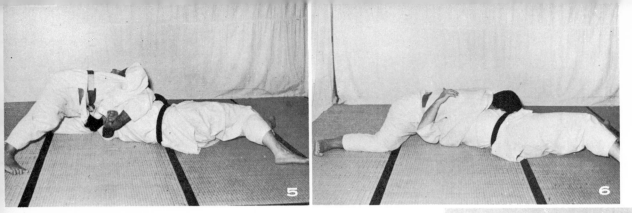

Figures 5–7. This is another modification in which the use of the arms is different. Reach around and under the opponent's neck with your left arm, catching it in the bend of the elbow. Also, bring your right arm over and under his right arm while maintaining a tight grip with your left arm. Both arms are pulling inward and clamping around the opponent's neck and shoulder like a vise. Sometimes this may produce strangulation although it is not intended to do so. Use your head to apply pressure to his abdomen when he tries to rise.

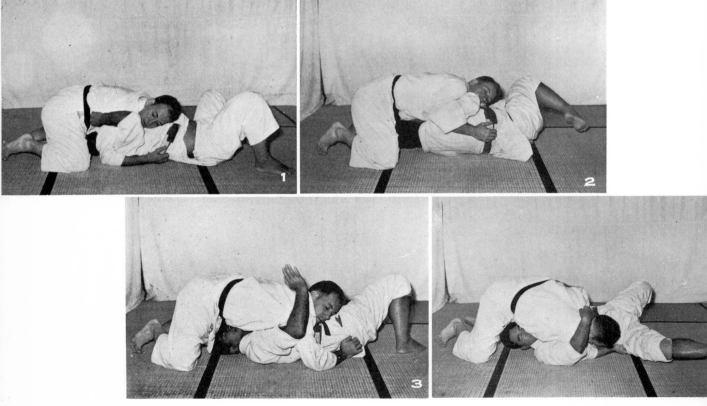

COUNTER TECHNIQUES FOR KAMI-SHIHO-GATAME

Figures 1-6. When the opponent applies this hold, it is not possible
to push him upward to escape. You can move on your back in the direction
of your head or feet and you can try to roll his body over, but do not
waste energy trying to push straight up. In this case, pull him forward
while moving back yourself. This brings his weight to the upper part of
his body which you hope to control. Bring your feet close to your buttocks
all the while for power in moving. Now, turning slightly to your left, work
your right hand back under his shoulder and out under his armpit. Reach
around his neck with your right arm and grasp his collar as far to the left
as possible, at the same time grip his belt with your left hand. Now turn
the opponent to your left by pulling with your right hand, pushing with
your left hand, and at the same time raising and turning your own body,
using your feet.

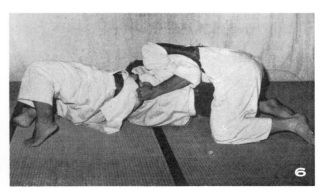

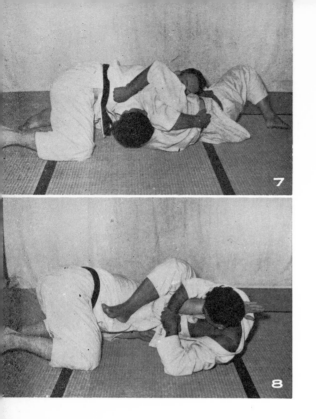

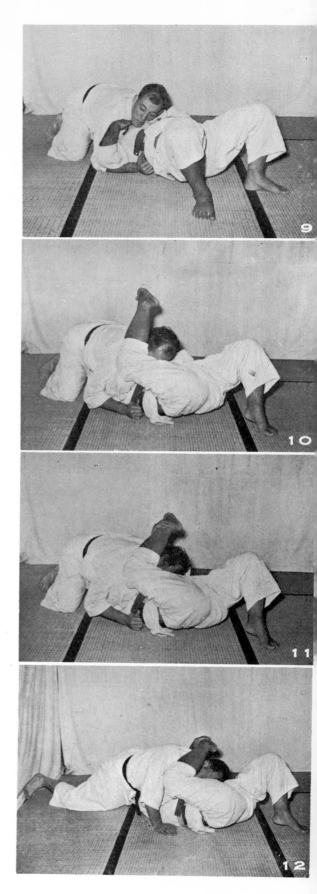

Figures 7-8. Move your body at an angle and bring your head out from under his right side by pushing with your feet and pulling with your arms. The opponent's position is now weak and you can escape or counter by applying an armlock as shown in the illustrations. In applying the armlock keep control of his right arm at all times.

Figures 9-12. Arch your back, then suddenly drop down. This will momentarily create a space between you and the opponent. Taking advantage of this opportunity, slide your right hand like a wedge under his neck, grasping his left collar. Now, bring your right leg back and over his neck, catching it in the bend of your knee. Grasp your right ankle with your left hand and pull down for pressure until your right forearm presses against his neck, strangling him. You may also catch your right ankle in the bend of your left leg behind the knee if you are supple enough.

kata-gatame: shoulder hold

Figures 1-4. This hold can be applied if you have control of the opponent's right arm after you have thrown him. Do not release your hold on his right arm, but push it slightly away from you and kneel down, your right knee near his armpit. With your left hand push his right arm up alongside his head, slide your right arm around his neck, and catch your right hand with your left. Clamp your arms together tightly and lower your forehead to the mat alongside his head. Keep your right knee tightly against his side with your left leg extending far out to the left. Remember you are weak toward your right shoulder, so keep control of his right arm and exert pressure toward your left front. Now you may change the position of your legs in order to lower your center of gravity. Sit down on the mat with your legs split as in a running position, right leg forward and left leg back. The pressure of your right forearm against his neck may cause strangulation.

Figures 5-6. Another way of pinning the opponent's shoulder is used when he starts to roll toward you, bringing his left arm across his body. Catch his left arm above his elbow under your left armpit. Slide your left hand deep under his neck, grasp his collar, and clamp his left arm tightly across his neck. Your right knee is brought into his side thus controlling his right arm and body, while your right arm is brought over his left side to hold his body close to you.

COUNTER-TECHNIQUES

Figures 7-8. As the opponent's force is at his front, it is easier to move him in that direction than in any other. Bring your feet close to your buttocks and bend your right arm, clenching the fist tightly. Contract your neck and concentrate all your strength in your upper body. Suddenly, arch your back and move two or three steps backward. This is done by pushing with your feet and straightening your right arm, contracting your body again, then repeating the pushing. Your form is similar to that of a snail. His forehead and hand will be pressed tightly and rubbed against the mat and cause him severe pain. The opponent will therefore loosen or release his hold, and you can escape.

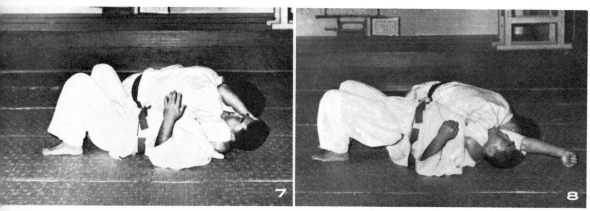

Figures 9-12. This next method is a little more complicated than most escapes, but with a little practice it can easily and successfully be executed. Place your left hand on your hip and raise your legs straight up as far as possible, bringing them back over your left shoulder and dropping down on your knees. With both hands grasp his right wrist tightly. Then do a split, bringing your right foot under you and sitting with both legs spread out. Upward pressure with your hands and downward pressure with your right shoulder will lock his right arm.

Figures 13-14. If the opponent does not have a strong hold on you, or if he stiffens his body, then you can easily sit up, pushing him over on his back. If the opponent is strong, first raise your legs, then quickly bring them down sitting up at the same time and pressing his right shoulder backward.

osaekomi-waza : 111

kesa-gatame: cross-chest hold

Kesa-gatame is one of the simplest holds to secure, especially after throwing the opponent as you still have control of his right arm. This move is not very strong because you are in a sitting position and your body is relatively easy for the opponent to control. However, it is possible to hold the opponent successfully, and your position allows you to change readily to strangulation or armlock techniques.

Sit alongside the opponent with your right side lying across his chest, and encircle his neck with your right arm. His right arm is secured tightly between your left arm and side as you grip his sleeve above the elbow. Expanding your chest also aids in clamping his arm to your side. Sit with your legs split, the right leg forward with the thigh under his right shoulder and the knee slightly bent. Your left leg is brought back behind you. This is important as you are weakest toward your back, and the left leg acts as a brace to prevent being tilted back. In order to control the opponent's upper body, it is necessary to raise his head so he cannot arch his back for escaping. This is done by raising his head with your right forearm or catching your right thigh with your right hand. The right thigh under his right shoulder is also an important controlling measure. As your back is your weakest point, the opponent will try to push you in that direction using his hands or to bring his left leg over across your neck. In order to avoid this, bend your head forward over his right shoulder. When the opponent tries to roll you to your right, put your right hand out on the mat to stop the roll. Remember to keep your body relaxed at all times and only apply pressure at the points of resistance when needed. Also, do not release his right arm at any time. If he manages to free his right arm and you cannot recover it, it is best to change your hold using another technique.

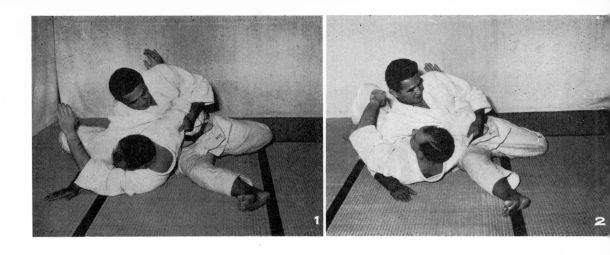

kuzure-kesa-gatame:
modified cross-chest hold

Figures 1-2. This technique is similar to *kesa-gatame*, except for the use of your right hand, which is kept under the opponent's armpit against his side. Because of the position of your right hand you are stronger to your right side, but he now has the free use of his left hand, which he can use against you. If he brings his left arm up against your neck to push you back, catch his arm with your right hand and hold it to the mat or apply an armlock.

Figures 3-5. When the opponent tries to roll you to your right, and you cannot maintain your balance, then come up on your right knee. Bringing your knee close to his body, swing your left leg over his head and sit back, applying an armlock to his right arm as shown in the illustrations.

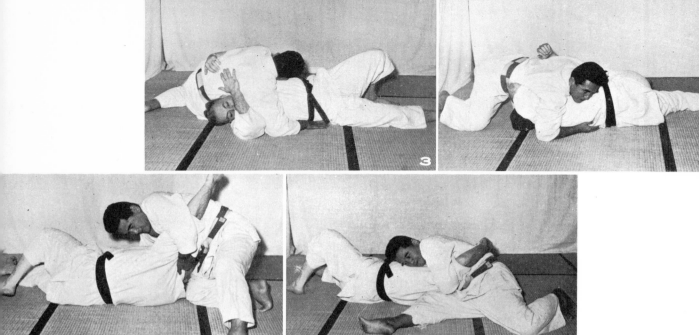

ushiro-kesa-gatame: rear cross-chest hold

Figures 1-6. This move may be described as a reverse *kesa-gatame*. Your body assumes approximately the same position as in *kesa-gatame* except that you lie across the opponent's chest from his shoulder to his waist. Because of your position, this move is considerably stronger than *kesa-gatame*. Although you still remain weak to your rear, it is difficult for him to push you in that direction.

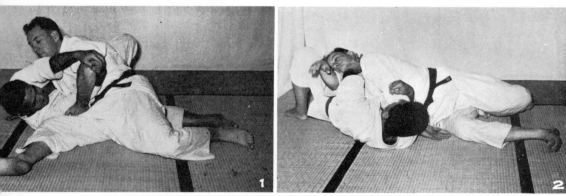

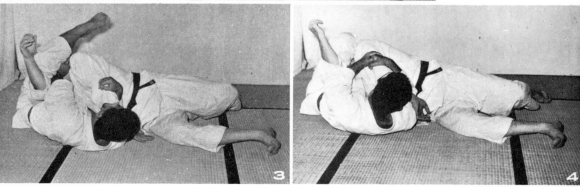

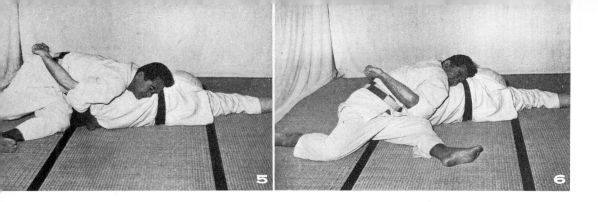

In this case, moreover, you have better control of his upper body. Catch his left arm above the elbow under your left armpit and lean across his shoulder with your right forearm along his right side. Grip his left arm tightly and hold your right arm firmly against his side, palm down. You may grasp his belt with your right hand for additional control when needed. Sit in a split position as in *kesa-gatame* with your right thigh under his left shoulder and left foot to the rear for balance. Keep your head along his side to prevent him from turning. Now if the opponent is strong and succeeds in turning his body to escape, you can easily change your position and apply the same move on the other side as shown in the illustrations. In this case he pulls his left arm out of your grip by rolling to his left side. Consequently, his right side is raised, and, switching to his right, you catch his right arm under your right armpit.

COUNTER-TECHNIQUES FOR KESA-GATAME

Figures 1-4. Turn your body so that your right shoulder touches the mat, thus creating a space between the two bodies. Grasping his right elbow on the outside with both hands, pull his elbow into you, bringing his forearm alongside your neck. Now push his head back at the neck with your left hand. Then, as he leans backward, bring your left leg across his neck, forcing him back still more. Throughout this operation, maintain control of his left elbow with your right hand. Now, placing your left hand on his elbow, arch your back and pull in with your hands, applying an armlock.

Figures 5-6. Another method of escaping and applying an armlock is as follows: freeing your right arm from his grip, push his left shoulder back, making him lean backward. At the same time keep control of his right arm, clamping it close to your side with the left arm. As the opponent is pushed backward, bring your left leg across his neck and grip above his right elbow with your right hand. Push away with your leg and pull in with your hands, applying an armlock (*ude-gatame*).

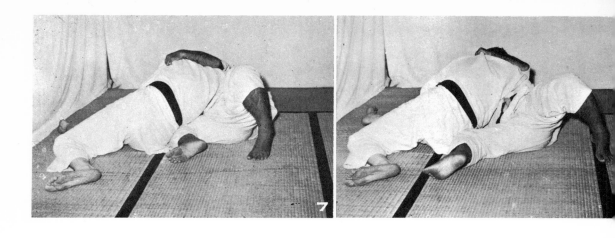

Figures 7-10. A basic principle in escaping from a hold is to try to create a space between you and the opponent. He can only control your body if it is close to him, but if there is a space then you can escape or counter him. This method shows a basic way of creating a space between you and the opponent. Slide your body to the left and turn on your right side, bringing your right knee up between you and his back. Work the knee under his side if possible. From this point you can easily turn him over by the use of your hands and legs. Notice how weak he is toward his rear. From the position shown in Figure 7, you can turn him over by pulling with your left hand and pushing up with your right hand and right leg. Now if the opponent lowers his head to counter your lifting force, push his body away further by using both legs. This will cause his right arm to become straight and powerless. Clamp his right arm to your side with your left arm as shown, and bring your left knee up, applying pressure to his elbow joint as you push away with your feet. This armlock is called *hiza-gatame.*

Figures 11-13. This is the simplest escape method from *kesa-gatame.* Move around to your right, trying to get your right knee under the opponent's side. He will move along with you in trying to retain his hold. As he moves forward he will have to raise his buttocks off the mat slightly. At this moment, just as he moves, grasp his belt with your left hand and turn him over on his back using leg power.

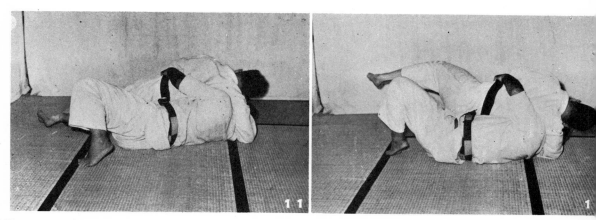

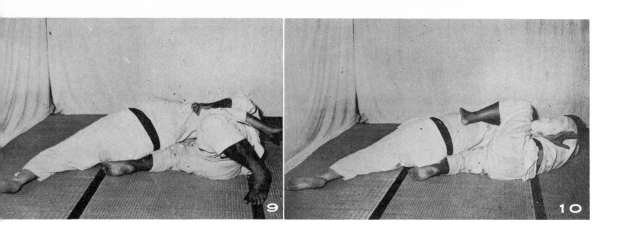

Figures 14-16. When the opponent holds you with *ushiro-kesa-gatame*, he is strong to his front but weak toward his left back shoulder. Grip the back of his jacket with your left hand and bring your feet back close to your buttocks. Push back strongly with your legs, while pulling him back with your left hand and pushing up with your right. As his body is straightened backward, roll over on your front, turning to the left, bringing your right leg over and touching the mat. From this position you may stand up or take the offensive on the mat.

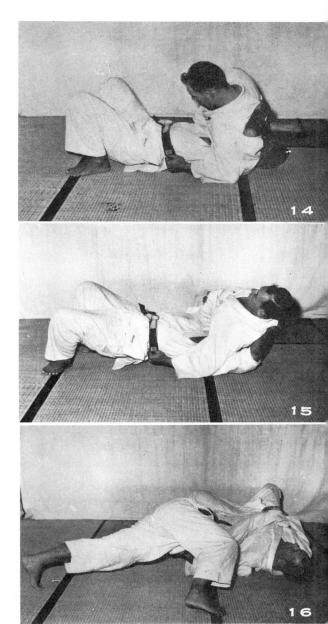

yoko-shiho-gatame: side four-corner hold

Figures 1-4. Bring your knees into his right side, touching his hip-joint and armpit. Put your left hand behind his neck and grasp the collar as deeply as possible. His right arm will now be under your left armpit where you can hold it tightly. Bring your right hand to his left side, reaching over his right thigh and under his left thigh, and grasp his belt. In this position his left thigh will be raised off the mat. Now press your chest against the right side of his chest, with your head applying pressure on his left chest. If the opponent tries to roll you over his left side, stretch your legs outward, shifting your center of gravity. However, if he still succeeds in pulling you over, stop this action by placing your forehead against the mat on his left side, then recover to your original position. As he attempts to escape, apply pressure with your chest and head against his chest, and pull in with your arms. Try to stay as relaxed as possible, only exerting pressure on the part of the body he tries to raise. If he tries to roll to his right side and appears successful, do not resist. But, as his left shoulder is raised, catch his left arm with your left arm, and, moving your body to his left side, apply *ushiro-kesa-gatame*. Then if he again rolls to his left side, you can grasp his right arm and apply *kesa-gatame*.

Figures 5-6. Another method of holding is to catch him with your right hand under his back by his belt or his clothes. Then suddenly lift up his buttocks with your right arm and bring your left leg under his back. Your right leg is behind you for support, and your chest presses against his chest. This method applies pressure to the opponent's neck and prevents him from escaping.

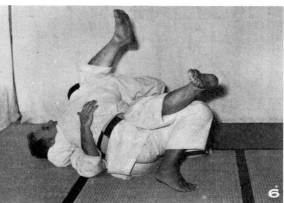

COUNTER-TECHNIQUES

Figures 7-8. The position of the opponent's left arm is relatively removed from his body, enabling you to control it successfully. Since your arms are free it is not difficult to control his left arm. Hence, press your head back, then catch his left elbow with both of your hands and press sideways, rolling to your left. You may now apply an armlock or escape.

Figures 9-12. Turn your body on your right side by wiggling slowly, then suddenly pull back. Work your right arm free and bring your right knee up between your body and his. Push away with your right knee and hands. His left arm is now out straight behind your neck. Now, cup your hands over his left elbow, drawing it into you, and at the same time bring your left knee over the top of his left shoulder. The pressure of your hands and the push of your legs will apply pressure to his elbow joint and he will submit.

tate-shiho-gatame: vertical four-corner hold

Figures 1-3. Sit on the opponent's abdomen with both knees touching the ground. Reach under his left armpit with your right arm and around his neck with your left arm. Cross both arms around the opponent as deep under as possible and hold tightly. Place your forehead on the mat just over his left shoulder. His left arm is now powerless. But he is in a position to roll you over. To prevent this, spread your knees and take both of your feet under his thighs, pressing his legs together. Your body should now be close to his from head to toe. If he can create a space between you and him, then he has a chance of escaping by bringing his leg up under your abdomen.

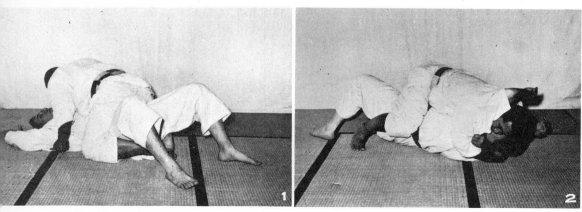

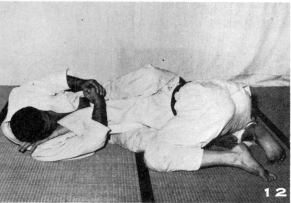

COUNTER-TECHNIQUES

Figures 4-6. Push his left leg down with your right hand and work your right knee back and under his thigh or abdomen. Then reach around his back with your left hand and grasp his left shoulder. Suddenly lift up his left leg with your right leg and hand and pull back across with your left hand. This will raise and roll his body over toward his left shoulder, which is his weak point.

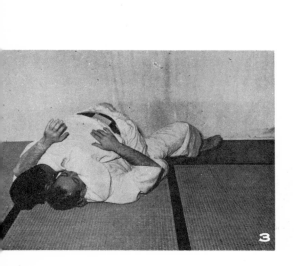

Figures 7-9. This method of escaping is similar to the above method except that you do not throw the opponent over you. Just raise him and roll him over slightly, while you roll out from under him in the opposite direction.

uki-gatame: *floating hold*

This method is best applied when you have thrown the opponent. Do not release your grip of his right arm, and, holding it tightly, catch his left shoulder with your right hand. Now with your weight on your left foot for balance, bring your right foot close to his right side and press your knee down diagonally across his abdomen. Keep your balance on your left foot and shift it to your right knee whenever it is necessary to apply pressure. The right knee should be free to move along his body, preventing him from raising any part of his lower body. Your hands control his upper body to prevent him from twisting or turning. His left arm can be controlled from the elbow with your right hand if necessary.

Escaping from this hold is accomplished merely by breaking off the connection from any part of his hold, then withdrawing your body.

CHAPTER **9**

shime-waza : strangling holds

Strangulation holds are effective means of subduing the opponent. They should not, however, be studied independently but in conjunction with other moves. Strangulation holds may be applied from either a standing or lying position, or from the front or rear. Strangulation is achieved by applying pressure to the jugular veins on either side of the neck. This cuts off the blood supply to the head and causes the opponent to faint without much pain. Pressure against the windpipe is not allowed and is dangerous. This is painful and only stops respiration. A person can retain consciousness much longer without air than without blood to the brain. In judo, if the opponent cannot escape from a strangulation hold he will clap his hands, stamp the mat with his hands or feet, or say *maitta* (surrender). At any of these signs of surrender, the opponent should be released immediately. If he blacks out, apply artificial respiration and he will regain consciousness without any harmful after-effects.

Most strangulation holds require that your hands enter deeply along the opponent's collar. Although strangulation holds may be forced, this usually meets with limited success and may only result in unnecessary injury. Since most people have an instinctive fear against strangulation, it is best to move into a strangulation hold in a natural manner without giving forewarnings of your intent. When you have worked your hands into position, apply pressure quickly and control the opponent's body by either unbalancing him if he is standing, or by pushing his lower body down with your feet if he is already lying down.

okuri-eri-jime: sliding collar choke

Figures 1-3. This is one of the simplest and strongest forms of choking, as it is only necessary to slide one hand alongside the opponent's neck and it is relatively difficult to escape from. When attacking from behind, slide your right thumb under the opponent's neck and catch his left collar deeply, thumb inside. Your inner wrist bone is against the side of his neck. Reach under his left armpit and grasp his right lapel with your left arm. Now, pull down on his right lapel and bring your right elbow back and around, thus choking him. When in a standing or sitting position, step back, turning to your right, thus breaking the opponent's balance to his rear and aiding the pull of your right arm. If you are in a lying position, wrap your legs around the opponent's waist and push his body down, arching your back as you do so. This stretches his body, increasing the pressure on his neck and preventing him from moving upward and escaping.

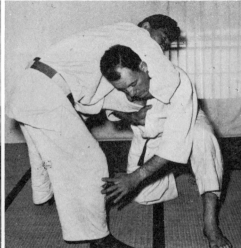

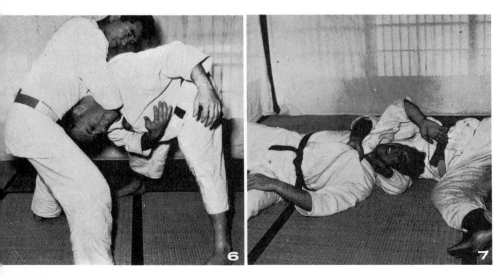

Figures 4-7. To apply the hold from the front, reach over his head and around the neck with your right hand, catching his right collar deeply. Now reach under his right armpit with your left arm and grasp his left lapel. To apply pressure, pull down with your left hand, up with your right arm, and push against his head with your abdomen. If the opponent falls to the mat in attempting to escape, fall with him, retaining your grip and applying pressure.

Figures 8-9. When you are applying the hold from the side and the opponent is on his hands and knees, kneel close to his body. If you are on his right side, bring your right hand under his neck, catching his left collar deeply. Then reach around the top of his back with your left hand, grasping his right lapel from underneath. Apply pressure by stepping in front of him with your left foot and sitting down while your arms apply pressure to his neck in the usual way. Keep moving to your left with your legs if the opponent tries to escape.

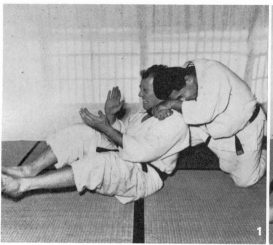

hadaka-jime: naked choke

This move does not utilize the opponent's clothing in achieving the hold. Only the attacker's bare arms are used.

Figure 1. When attacking from the rear, slip your right hand, palm down, deeply around the opponent's neck. Grasp your right hand with your left hand and pull back, pressing your head against the side of the opponent's head. Bring your right elbow back as you choke him.

Figure 2. This application is the same as the previous one except for the use of your left arm. Catch your right hand above the bend in your left arm and bring the palm of your left hand behind the opponent's head. Press his head forward as you apply the choke.

Figures 3-5. When applying this move from the front, use your hands as originally described. However, push your abdomen against his head to apply pressure. If the opponent drops to the mat, then place your feet on his hips and apply pressure by pushing his body away.

kataho-jime: half side choke

Figure 1. When attacking from the rear, slide your right hand, thumb inside, around his neck, grasping his left collar deeply. Bring his left arm up and lock it by placing your left hand behind his neck. Push his head forward as you apply pressure with your right hand. This move is similar to *okuri-eri-jime*.

Figures 2–3. When the opponent is on all fours, and you are at his right side, reach under his neck with your right hand and catch his collar deeply. Bring your right foot over the front of his right arm and grasp the inside of his left sleeve with your left hand. Drop down, hooking his right arm with your right leg, and stretch your body outward as you push his left arm out from under him. At the same time bring up your right elbow, thus choking him.

Figures 4–5. Another method is to grasp his left collar as before, but to cross your left hand over your right forearm, pressing the back of your hand against his face. Curve your fingers backward against his cheek so that he cannot turn his head and escape.

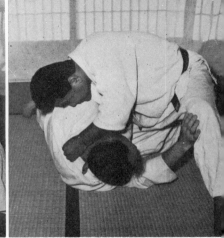

juji-jime: cross chokes

In this technique, strangulation is accomplished by crossing your arms and gripping the opponent's collar with both hands. There are three general types of cross chokes, the only difference being in the way the hands grip the collar.

1. *Kata-juji-jime:* half cross choke. One palm up and the other down.
2. *Nami-juji-jime:* natural cross choke. Both palms up.
3. *Gyaku-juji-jime:* reverse cross choke. Both palms down.

When applying pressure with a cross choke, pull in with your arms, spreading your elbows and pressing the side of your head against the opponent. If you are in a lying position, then place your feet on the opponent's hips and push his lower body away as you choke, stretching his body and increasing the pressure on his neck. This also keeps him from moving up and escaping.

Figures 1-4 (*kata-juji-jime:* half cross choke). As soon as the opponent is thrown down, maintain control over his right arm and kneel at his right side with your right knee into his armpit. Slide your right hand, palm up, deep inside his right collar and bear down on his shoulder with your forearm. Now the opponent cannot raise his right shoulder to escape, but his left arm is free. He will therefore roll toward you, trying to escape. At this moment his left shoulder is raised and it is easy for you to grasp his left collar, palm down, with your left hand. Do so and lie down on your

left side, crossing your forearms under his neck. He will naturally roll on top of you, trying to get up. Let him do so, and at that moment, pull in with your arms and push his hips away with your feet, thereby strangling him. In this move you appear to let the opponent have his way, putting him off guard, giving you a good chance to place your hands in position.

Figures 5-8 (*kata-juji-jime:* half cross choke). In this case the opponent attacks you from the front. Hold him off with your feet against his hips. Reach up and slide your right hand, palm up, under his right collar and catch the back of his collar, palm down, with your left hand. Draw his body into you and cross your left forearm over and under his neck. Suddenly push away with your feet on his hips and draw your arms in tightly, spreading the elbows.

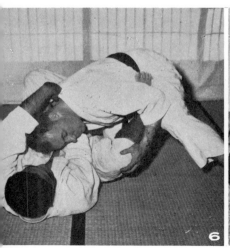

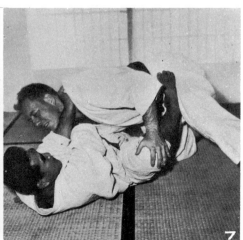

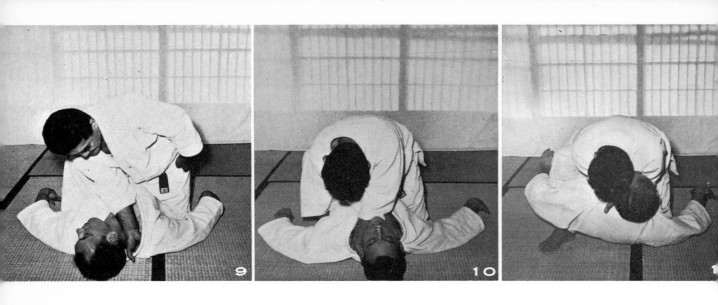

Figures 12-14 (*nami-juji-jime:* natural cross choke). Entering from the opponent's right side, grasp the back of his right collar deeply, palm down, with your right hand. As you straddle the opponent's body, grasp his left back collar, palm down, with your left hand. Quickly pull up and choke. If the opponent struggles and rolls you over, do not resist, but roll with him. At this moment push his hips down with your feet. This will make his body drop low, and his own weight will add power to your hold.

Figures 9-11 (*gyaku-juji-jime:* reverse cross choke). Straddling the opponent's body, slip your hands one at a time, palms up, deeply under his collar. In fact, try to have the hands touch each other at the back of his collar if possible. Choke by raising the opponent's head and spreading your elbows.

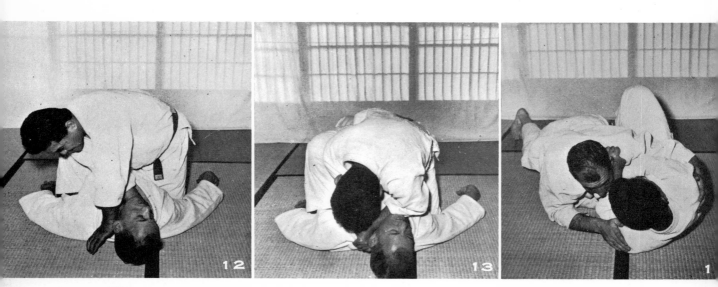

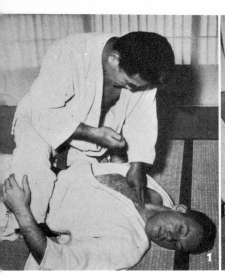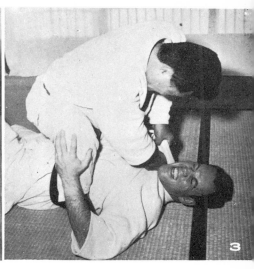

tsukikomi-jime: poking choke

This technique effects strangulation from the front by pressure of the right index-finger knuckle against the opponent's right jugular vein just above the collarbone.

Figures 1-3. Hold both of the opponent's lapels, thumbs inside, and pull forward. Next, still gripping the lapels, bring his left lapel across to his right side, placing your right index-finger knuckle against the pressure point (Figure 1). Strangle by pushing in with your knuckle and pulling his right lapel forward and slightly across to your right.

Figures 4-6. This application varies only in the use of the opponent's right lapel. Both lapels are gripped in your right hand. The knuckle is placed against his neck, and you pull his right lapel through your right hand with your left. This is the same action as a noose around his neck, and the pulling of the lapel through your hand draws his collar tightly around his neck.

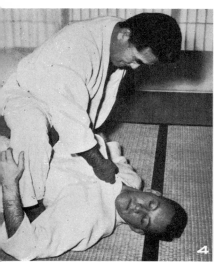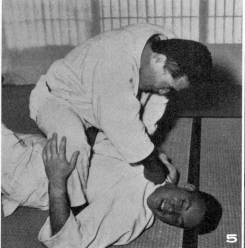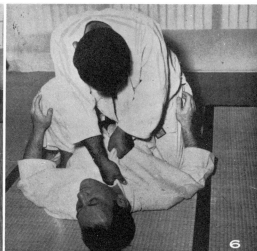

  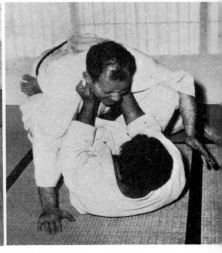

ryote-jime: both hands choke

This move is easily applied from a standing or lying position. Grasp deeply with both hands, palms down, each side of the opponent's collar, the right hand on his left side and the left on his right side. At first hold the collar loosely so as not to arouse his suspicion as to what you intend to do. Once in position, apply pressure by turning your hands and elbows inward and up, with the knuckles of both hands pressing tightly into the front sides of his neck. Press in and up against the jugular veins just above the collar bones. When lying down, place your feet against the opponent's hips and push down. If standing up, raise your body up and forward, bringing your abdomen forward.

sode-guruma-jime: lapel wheel choke

As you approach the opponent from behind, reach over his right shoulder with your left arm and grasp his left lapel, palm down. Pull his left lapel up across the neck and, at the same time, reach over his left shoulder with your right hand and grasp his jacket in front of the shoulder. Apply pressure by pulling back and spreading your elbows.

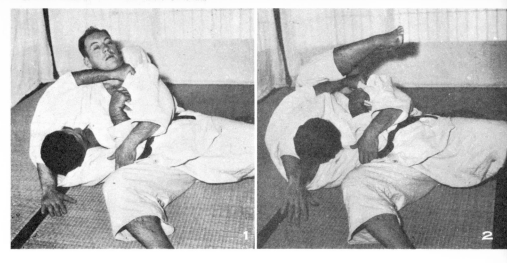

kesa-gatame-jime: *cross-chest choke*

When the opponent holds you with *kesa-gatame*, he is weak toward his rear, and your left hand is free. Reach across with your left hand, thumb inside, grasping his left collar and pushing him backward. Release your right hand and pull his left lapel through your left hand, drawing his collar tightly around his neck. At the same time bring your left leg up and across his head. Choke by pulling in with your left arm and pushing away with your leg.

counter-techniques for shime-waza

When a choke hold is applied, usually only one hand does the actual strangling, while the other acts as a counter-force which applies pressure in the opposite direction. You must control the strangling arm in order to relieve the pressure on your neck. The natural tendency is to panic and to move against the opponent's hands to force your way free. This is just what he wants, and a wild struggle will cause the strangulation to be more effective. Therefore, relax and, moving slowly but surely, determine your course of action and follow it through. Remember you have almost thirty seconds before you blackout, and that if you pull down on the choking arm and relieve the pressure you will not blackout.

Figures 1-2. When the opponent applies a choke from the rear such as *okuri-eri-jime* escape as follows: grip his right arm (strangling arm) with your hands at the elbow and forearm and pull down, relieving the pressure. Now, still pulling, turn your head to the right and push his elbow up, thus removing your head from the hold.

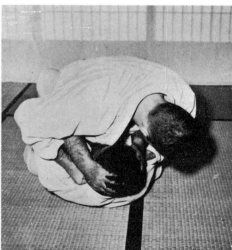

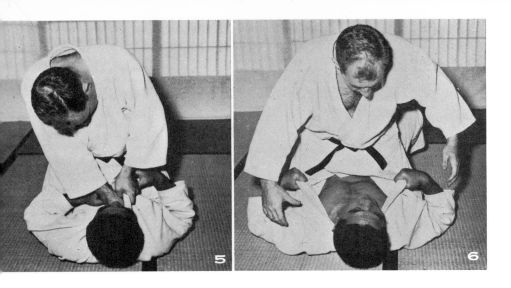

Figure 3. When the opponent applies *juji-jime* his top arm usually effects the strangulation. Therefore, push up on his top elbow and roll your head in that direction to escape.

Figure 4. If the opponent applies *ryote-jime*, drive both of your hands up between his, catching your head in your hands. Then, spread your elbows and his hands will be pushed away from your neck.

Figures 5-6. When the opponent applies *tsukikomi-jime*, merely grip your lapels and pull them apart quickly.

Figures 7-8. To escape from *sode-guruma-jime*, catch your left lapel with both hands and jerk it down hard.

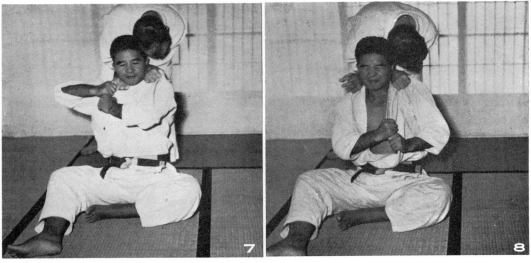

CHAPTER *10*

kansetsu-waza:
armlock techniques

$a$rmlock techniques are usually applied in conjunction with other moves, but they may be applied directly. In judo, you are allowed to apply pressure only to the elbow joint. Pressure on any other joint is considered dangerous, as it can easily result in permanent injury. The elbow joint can take a lot of pressure, and it is very painful before the breaking point is reached. The opponent will therefore surrender and in most cases will not suffer from any aftereffects other than a possible soreness. However, as this is only a sport, pressure should be applied gradually in order to prevent injury. Pressure is applied directly against the elbow when the arm is straight or indirectly when it is bent.

ude-garami: coil armlock

This move is applied by bending the opponent's arm at an angle, then applying a counter-force against the elbow. You have probably seen this many times as a form of self-defense in disarming an aggressor. It can be applied from a standing or lying position.

Figure 1. The opponent is on his back, and you are kneeling at his right side. As he raises his left arm, catch it at the wrist with your left hand, palm down, and bend it back to the mat. You are now lying across his chest, and his arm is bent up at a 90 degree angle. Bring your right hand, palm down, under his left arm slightly above the elbow and grasp your left wrist. Apply pressure to the elbow by twisting his wrist in and down with your left hand and by raising your right elbow. It is easier to exert pressure if his arm is only a quarter bent (approximately 45 degrees), as the arm is weaker in that position.

Figures 2 & 3. These illustrations show the same move being applied in different positions. Notice that you can also apply this move with the opponent's arm bent down as well as when it is bent upward.

COUNTER-TECHNIQUES

The general method of escape is to turn around quickly in the direction in which your arm is being twisted. Suppose the opponent lies across your body and grasps your left arm as in Figure 1. Quickly work your right hand under his body and grip the right side of his jacket. Exert some pressure with your left hand and resist his application so that you are able to stretch the arm a little. Suddenly push up his body with your right hand, slipping under his body at the same time. The passage for your escape is the space below his waist. Turn your head and shoulder to the left so that it resists the opponent's action and pull your arm out of the lock.

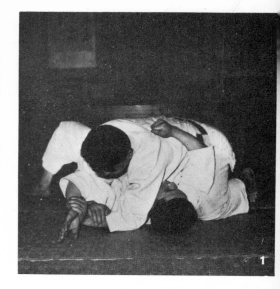

ude-gatame: straight armlock

This move is applied when the opponent's arm is straight. Usually your opponent tries to catch your collar to push you away or, if you are standing, to throw you.

Figure 1. The opponent reaches for your right collar trying to push you away with his left hand. Just as he reaches, lower your body a little so that his hand passes over your right shoulder alongside your neck. Bend forward, catching his wrist between your neck and shoulder; also cup both of your hands over the outside of his elbow. Your body should be close to his with one knee raised for balance. To apply pressure, straighten your body, stomach forward, and roll your right shoulder toward the front and press in his elbows with both hands.

Figure 2. Lie across the opponent, stretching his left arm out straight, with your left hand gripping his wrist. Slide your right arm under his elbow and grip your own left arm near the elbow. Apply pressure by raising your right elbow up and pushing down with your left hand.

Figures 3-4. This is an application of the same move except that in this case the opponent is over you, attempting a hold, and places his right hand by your left shoulder. Catch the back of his elbow with both hands. Press the elbow in with your hands as you push his lower body down and away with your feet. This straightens his arm, and the counter pressure of the forward push of your left shoulder and the inward pull of your hands will lock the arm.

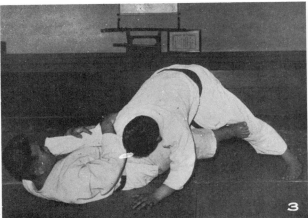

Figures 5-6. When the opponent grabs your left collar with his right hand from a standing position, catch his wrist between your neck and shoulder. Then bring your left hand under and around and place your palm on his elbow. Cup your right hand over your left. Apply pressure by raising your left shoulder and drawing in with your hands.

COUNTER-TECHNIQUES

The opponent must have his hands over your elbow to apply pressure. Therefore push your arm forward, making the position of his hands move to a point away from the elbow. Then turn your elbow, bending it slightly, and quickly withdraw your arm. When in a standing position, you must do a forward summersault to escape.

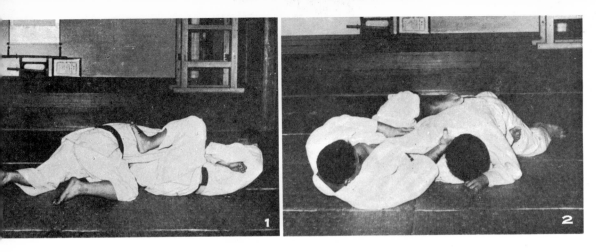

hishigi-hiza-gatame: arm-knee lock

This hold is similar to *ude-gatame* except that in this case you use your knee for pressure on the elbow joint.

The opponent is on your right side attempting a hold and places his right hand under or near your left armpit. Bring your left arm over his, holding his arm against your left side with the palm of your left hand over his elbow. Grip his collar with your right hand to keep him from moving away. Then place your right foot on his left thigh and push away, stretching his body out flat. With your left foot on his right hip, turn your knee in against the elbow, applying pressure. (See Figure 3 for a variation of this hold.)

COUNTER-TECHNIQUES

If you cannot pull your hand out, and his feet are placed in position, push his right thigh in with your left hand. This will take his foot off your left thigh. Then roll your body to the left, moving upward and pulling your arm out.

juji-gatame: cross lock

This technique is highly versatile and can be applied under many circumstances. For example, after you throw your opponent, stand by his right side, holding his right arm. Catch his right wrist tightly with both of your hands and pull up. Then suddenly drop down, with your buttocks as close to his side as possible, simultaneously bringing your left leg over his neck or shoulders. It is important to keep pulling his right arm as you drop down into position, and to bring your knees inward, holding his arm tightly between your thighs. Your right leg is bent deeply, with the foot wedged under his body. To apply pressure, pull his right arm and arch your back, raising your abdomen and squeezing in with your thighs. The upward pressure of the abdomen and the downward pull on his wrist create opposite forces and apply pressure on the elbow. Move into position quickly, otherwise he will pull his arm away. You can also use this move while attempting to apply a hold. As the opponent tries to escape, he will sometimes push you away with his arm. At that time grasp his wrist and swing your body into position, applying the hold as originally described. This shows the importance of being able to apply armlocks, for during close in-fighting, the opponent will invariably try to push you away with his arms. As his arm is straightened, it loses its strength and it is easy for you to apply an armlock. Another application of this move was shown under the counter-techniques for *tai-otoshi*.

COUNTER-TECHNIQUES

It is necessary that you escape from an armlock before the opponent applies pressure. Just as the opponent starts to lie on his back, twist your hand a little, bend your elbow, and pull your hand down with force. Pull in the direction of his front pelvic bone, so that the elbow can be drawn toward your right ribs. If you are lying on your back at that time, you will not be able to withdraw your arm. Therefore, as you pull the arm, turn on your right side. If the opponent is strong and you cannot pull out your arm, then catch your right hand with your left hand and pull your arm out using both hands.